It was in Sandy's most difficult time in her life that we became friends. I witnessed first hand the power of God working in the life of this precious lady as she came face to face with the greatest pain—the loss of a daughter. *Remembering Laura* powerfully tells the story of God's grace in our most dire time of need. I simply want to shout, 'READ this book! It will encourage your heart in our great God!'

—Kendall Lucas, worship pastor, Denton
Bible Church, Denton, Texas.

This beautifully written story is a profound reminder we can face anything with enduring faith. Sandy's pen went straight to my heart, writing hope all over it.

—Debbie Graham, Bible study teacher, author, conference leader, founder Heart Hugs International,
former television host, Lenexa, Kansas.

In *Remembering Laura*, Sandy captivates my heart with her eloquently written words of her daughter's beautiful but brief life. It is a true labor of love and an inspiring journey of grief and hope.

—Vicki Garrett Harmon, life-long, dear friend
of Laura K, New Bern, North Carolina.

Remembering Laura is not a story of death, but of *living*! It is about praising God with even the very last breath you take. Sandy said it best in this precious book, 'Even though the journey was not ending as we had prayed that it would, God was still God.' He changed our lives with an *angel*, Laura.

—Paige Kraus, Vice President of Laura's Legacy Foundation, precious friend of Laura K.

Upon opening *Remembering Laura*, you will be compelled to read every word from cover to cover in one sitting. You will fall in love with Laura, the golden girl with a mega-watt smile and a passion for embracing every single moment of life. She was a young woman who demonstrated what it means to walk through the *valley* with joy intact and faith unshaken because she knows Jesus, the Great Shepherd who sustains forever. When you close the book, you will grasp anew the clarity of the timeless words of the 23rd Psalm, and you will want to know this Great Shepherd as Laura knows him.

—Christy Selvidge, children's ministry leader, First Baptist Church, Fort Lauderdale, Florida.

If you ever wonder where to turn during life's great challenges, *Remembering Laura* is a must read. This story is a beautiful example of how Christ's love can lift us up and carry us through our most difficult trials.

—Dr. Nathan Strandmark, physician, Garden City, Kansas.

Remembering
Laura

Remembering
Laura
letting go of life with beauty and grace

Sandy Badgett

TATE PUBLISHING & *Enterprises*

Scripture quotations marked "NIV" are taken from the *Holy Bible, New International Version* ®, Copyright © 1973, 1978, 1984 by International Bible Society. Used by permission of Zondervan Publishing House. All rights reserved.

Scripture quotations marked "NASB" are taken from the *New American Standard Bible* ®, Copyright © 1960, 1962, 1963, 1968, 1971, 1972, 1973, 1975, 1977, 1995 by The Lockman Foundation. Used by permission. All rights reserved.

Scripture quotations marked "NKJV" are taken from *The New King James Version* / Thomas Nelson Publishers, Nashville: Thomas Nelson Publishers. Copyright © 1982. Used by permission. All rights reserved.

Scripture quotations marked "NLT" are taken from the *Holy Bible, New Living Translation*, Copyright © 1996. Used by permission of Tyndale House Publishers, Inc. All rights reserved.

The opinions expressed by the author are not necessarily those of Tate Publishing, LLC.

Published by Tate Publishing & Enterprises, LLC
127 E. Trade Center Terrace | Mustang, Oklahoma 73064 USA
1.888.361.9473 | www.tatepublishing.com

Tate Publishing is committed to excellence in the publishing industry. The company reflects the philosophy established by the founders, based on Psalm 68:11,
"The Lord gave the word and great was the company of those who published it."

Book design copyright © 2009 by Tate Publishing, LLC. All rights reserved.
Cover design by Amber Lee
Interior design by Nathan Harmony
Author photograph by Janelle Vano
Edited by Angela Faulkner

Published in the United States of America

ISBN: 978-1-60799-078-9
1. Religion: Christian Life: Inspirational
2. Family & Relationships: Death, Grief, Bereavement
09.05.07

Dedication

Remembering Laura is dedicated to Laura's two little blonde-haired, blue-eyed boys; Colin, who has his mommy's face, and Cooper, who has his mommy's heart, with the hope and prayer that they might always remember their mother, Laura.

"We remember…your endurance inspired by hope" (1 Thessalonians 1:3, NIV).

and

"Her children arise and call her blessed" (Proverbs 31:28, NIV).

Acknowledgment

I must begin by offering words of thanks and appreciation to all those who have guarded and shepherded our hearts through these last long years. God gathered around us, during this long season of loss and grief, such a chorus of individuals who daily offered prayers on our behalf. I will be forever grateful and pray I might always be that source of encouragement for others as well. I also offer my thanks to all who extended a hand and a heart to me and to our families, in ways both big and small. Not one act of kindness went unnoticed—not one. I have appreciated—our families have appreciated—every prayer that was offered, every meal that was prepared, every thought that was expressed, and the many and unique ways in which each one of you showed how very much you cared. From our heart to yours, thank you.

The support we received from the people of Garden City was immeasurable. How very much this one young life touched this one small community. To John's family and the extended Kleysteuber family, to our own families, to our close circle of friends, to our church families, people we have known and loved, and friends we have never met, you have each touched our hearts deeply by touching Laura's heart. Thank you.

To Joe, for loving and walking beside me for nearly forty years and for being the godly man that you are; to Matt and Thomas, for being such amazing sons and brothers and uncles. God blessed me with exactly what I had prayed for—two strong sons and a beautiful daughter. To Karen, so newly added to our family—how grateful I am for your presence in my life; to John and Cooper and Colin, you are each loved so very much. Laura is so very proud of you and the strength and courage you have shown, for the men you are and the young men you are becoming. Thank you each for the joy you have added to our lives.

To Donnie Simpson, for his words of affirmation in the foreword and to my chorus of endorsers, people whom I have loved dearly. To Gail Stroup, who unselfishly offered her editing and formatting expertise (you are so very talented in so very many ways). To Jim and Janell Davis, for the vision they have had to encourage me in my writing efforts and to see beyond simply a book in the years ahead. To my dear friends who offered to sharpen my pencils, supply cokes, or brings flowers. To Scott Badgett, for helping make the connection with Tate Publishing. (God had been carefully orchestrating that moment for over thirty years.) And to Dr. Richard Tate and Tate Publishing for having the confidence to take this step of faith with me and to make the process so easy. Thank you each. You have lightened the burden of the journey and helped me to shoulder the grief.

And finally, but foremost of all, thank you to God for dreaming of a plan that would offer Laura and us all the free gift of salvation and an eternity in heaven; to his one and only Son, Jesus, for teaching us daily how to live; and to his Holy Spirit, who indwells us and whispers to us how we are to move forward ... *you* never left our side. *You* never left Laura's side, not even for a moment. "Thanks be to God for his indescribable gift" (2 Corinthians 9:15, NIV).

Table of Contents

Foreword

If we are fortunate, our lives are not rocked often by tragedy, but when tragedy does happen—and it will happen—where do we turn? In those moments when God doesn't make sense and your life has been changed forever, where do *you* turn?

Remembering Laura will help you find hope for the future in knowing God is always at work in your life, even in the midst of life's most difficult times. You will be encouraged to live each day to the fullest, when life is good and when life is so very hard.

When parents dream dreams for their children, they envision long, rewarding, and fulfilling days and years. No parent expects to outlive a child. That is just not the natural order of life. Yet, that is the journey my dear friends, Joe and Sandy Badgett have had to endure.

My wife, Dava, and I met the Badgett family over twenty years ago. We have been fortunate to be a part of their family and have been blessed by their friendship. Our families have celebrated the joyous times and have walked together through the valleys. I am humbled that the Badgett family refers to me as their "personal pastor." I consider it a privilege to minister to such a wonderful Christian family.

I was asked to officiate the wedding of their daughter, Laura, in 1998. We were all so excited that day as John and Laura became husband and wife. Laura was a lovely young lady and a beautiful bride, and I was honored and excited to be a part of this celebration of marriage. Little did I know that the lines they repeated that day as a part of their wedding vows "in sickness and in health…until death do us part" would come into play just two years later.

The next five years forever changed the life of Laura and the lives of her family and friends as she was diagnosed with brain cancer. I remember sitting for hours with the family at the hospital numerous times as this part of their life's journey played out. Frustrated that there were not words adequate enough to relieve them of this pain they were now enduring and knowing, my presence and my prayers were all I had to offer.

As Laura's earthly journey came to an end and God took her home, I was asked to speak one more time, at Laura's memorial service. To honor one you loved like a daughter and to stand before your closest friends offering comfort in their moment of grief was a humbling challenge. But, as you will see through each page of this book, it is by the grace of God that we are sustained in those most difficult times.

Sandy Badgett is a woman of strong faith who has written of the unplanned journey of her family. Sandy's lovely daughter, Laura, fought what would prove to be a losing battle with brain cancer. As someone who has lived the peaks and valleys of one of the tragedies of life, Sandy writes with great compassion from the heart of a loving mother. Her many years in ministry and her years of experience serving on the staff of several large churches have given her unique preparation for this arduous journey. However, it is her relationship with God that sustains her. She writes of events along the way that shaped the steps that she took, but she directs us, always, to the one who shaped the events.

—Donnie Simpson, Director of Area Missions, SBC, Kansas City, Kansas, Baptist Association.

I want to leave a legacy...how will they remember me?

—Nichole Nordeman

Preface

We remember a young woman of great beauty and incredible grace. Her name was Laura Kleysteuber. She was John's faithful and beautiful wife. She was Cooper and Colin's loving mommy. She was Joe's adoring daughter. She was Matt and Thomas' little, big, and sometimes annoying sister. She was Vicki's, and so many others,' dear friend. And she was my baby girl. Webster's Dictionary[1] has this to say about *grace*, "a disposition to kindness and compassion; elegance and beauty." That was Laura K. She walked through life clothed in a beauty and grace that came as a gift from her heavenly father, and she did so always with a wink and a smile.

This is not a story I "purposed" to write. However, I believe it is a story God wants to be told. Several years ago, early in Laura's journey, I sensed God first whispering to my heart that this book would one day be written. I carefully pushed the thought to the very deepest, darkest part of my brain and my heart for I knew the journey that would need to be taken for me to do so, and it was a path I did not want to take. However, I also knew how God uses the stirrings in our heart to communicate critical messages to us, so I listened. The words began as a series of e-mails I composed for family and friends who were far away from us, after long days of care-giving throughout the summers and winters of 2005–2006. I believe that God first began writing these words on my heart during each of those long days. Throughout the months and years that have followed, I have simply tried to untangle the threads of this story so that the truths of those moments might make sense for someone who is hurting today. As Nicol Sponberg[2] pleads in her song, "Resurrection," "make something beautiful out of all this suffering." That is the desire of my heart. In perhaps the same way he once inspired the Old Testament writers, I very humbly believe God has burdened my heart to "Write in a book all the words that I will tell you" (Jeremiah 30:1, NIV). We pray that God might continue to use Laura's story to encourage others, to offer hope, and to draw people unto himself.

In Nichole Nordeman's beautiful song "Legacy,"[3] she writes, "I want to leave a legacy, how will they remember me? Did I choose to live, did I point to you? I want to leave a mark on things, want to leave an offering; child of mercy and grace, who blessed your name, unapologetically, to leave that kind of legacy."

Our memories of Laura resonate with the moments of faith, love, and laughter that filled every day of her life. She has indeed left a powerful legacy. She died much too soon at the age of thirty after a very long battle with brain cancer, but she will be remembered always.

Laura loved to run and knew the importance of keeping herself strong physically, emotionally, and spiritually so she could fight the cancer that had invaded her body. We watched, as even in her very last days, she ran with such strength and courage; it amazed us all. She never allowed the cancer or the treatments to keep her from the things that were most important to her—loving her family, bringing glory and honor to God, spending precious moments with friends, and bringing joy to those around her.

God blessed Laura with a beautiful face, and people were always struck by her incredible beauty, not just her outward beauty, which was clearly evident, but a deep inner beauty that came from within her heart. However, if you had questioned her about her beauty, she would have denied it. Laura simply loved being a wife and a mother and knew how very blessed she was. She was known for her "wink and a smile" approach to life. People were drawn to that smile and the kindness of her heart. Joy and laughter followed her everywhere, even in her very last days.

Laura would want you to know that she was not perfect. She made mistakes, she missed opportunities, she had flaws, but she loved a perfect God. This is not really Laura's story, or even my story. It is, as Louie Giglio[4] has said, the story of God, and these are just a few of the moments that have included all of us.

Finally, she would want you to know, and to remember, that God is at work in the story of your life as well. If you watch for his hand, you will see it profoundly and powerfully there. Our prayer, her prayer, is that you will. And so, we remember.

We had to remember. To do anything less would deny what God had
already done.

Remembering the Early Days of Cancer

"We continually remember before our God and Father your work produced by faith, your labor prompted by love, and your endurance inspired by hope" (1 Thessalonians 1:3, NIV).

In those early days after Laura's death, I prepared a list of **Ten Things I Remember About My Mommy** as a gift for her two little boys, Colin and Cooper, for Christmas that first year. They were only two and four when their mommy left this earth, and I knew how very important it would be to keep the few real, personal memories alive in their heads and hearts. It was a very simple list that a two and a four-year-old could easily understand:

Ten Things I Remember About My Mommy

1. My mommy loved me very much. And she loved my daddy too.
2. My mommy loved to laugh. Her beautiful smile brought joy and laughter to every room.
3. My mommy liked to eat popcorn with us in our fort in the backyard.
4. My mommy loved to play peek-a-boo.
5. My mommy loved to read stories at bedtime; we had fun playing in our tent and playing "corn" with our farm trucks.
6. My mommy liked to "shoot" birds from the front porch with our squirt guns.
7. My mommy loved to take walks and ride bikes and swim at our pool.
8. My mommy loved our little yellow house, and she made it a beautiful home for us all.
9. My mommy loved God and taught us about heaven too.
10. My mommy loved me very, very, very much.

That framed print still sits on the boys' dresser in their room, and I pray that it will for many years so that they may read and remember.

Webster's Dictionary[5] uses these words to describe the word *remember*: "to recall to mind by an act or effort of memory, to think of again. To retain in the memory; to remain aware of. To have something, or someone, come to mind again. To have recollections. To recall to the mind with effort; to think of again." To remember. To recall. To reflect. How could we ever forget? We will always remember Laura's beauty, her smile, and her endurance, which was inspired by the hope that she embraced.

Laura's diagnosis came in July of 2000. She had not even been married two years. It was an absolutely beautiful summer day in Garden City, Kansas, and Laura, John, and his family had spent the afternoon at the neighborhood pool. Laura loved afternoons like this—the pool, the water, a gathering of family and friends—the setting for a perfect afternoon. Everyone in John's very large family was in town for the wedding of John's cousin, Nathan Strandmark. Laura had driven John into town to prepare for his role in the wedding, and she was headed back to the pool to pick up the rest of the family. She was just a few blocks from her home and their neighborhood pool when the very first seizure hit. I wonder even today if she had any foreknowledge of what was to come. She had experienced a long season of headaches in college, which we thought were all related to those late-night studies or her need for glasses, but perhaps it had been something more. Did her vision change as she approached the pool? When did the trembling of the seizure begin? Did she know what was happening, or was she aware at all?

What we do know is that remarkably God allowed her to maintain control of their Suburban and herself until she was in the parking lot of the pool and had safely thrown the car's transmission into park. By the time John's family reached her, she had completely turned her body around in the seat so that she was facing backwards. She was in that "quiet place" between being fully conscious and not. She was aware yet not fully aware. Confused and sleepy. Still wearing her swimsuit from the afternoon of swimming, the medical team that was called to the scene said immediately that she was probably simply dehydrated from being out in the sun all afternoon. I am sure they surveyed her long, lean body, toned and strong from her frequent runs and daily workouts, and simply thought she had succumbed to the near one hundred degree heat. They took her to the hospital, administered fluids, and sent her home, telling her that she really had nothing to worry about. *Nothing to worry about.*

Laura and John were living in western Kansas in the little yellow house that they had just finished building that summer. They had met and fallen in love at Kansas State University and had been married in 1998. John, a fourth-generation farmer/rancher, had brought his beautiful bride home there to live and to grow deep roots in Garden City, Kansas. She had. She fully embraced both the love and the life that had brought her to this western most region of Kansas nearly six and a half hours from her parents and brothers and the Kansas City area, which she also dearly loved.

That day in July, Laura came home from the hospital and rested in her bed and wondered what had happened. She called her dad and me on the phone and simply said in a quiet voice, "I had a seizure today." It was almost like a question. *The strangest thing happened today.* What could it all mean? A CT scan was done at the hospital, and the young technician who reviewed her images said that he saw nothing to be concerned about, perhaps a small area of bruising. He specifically said, "There is no tumor." Still John and Laura were unsettled by the events of the weekend, as were we all, and made the decision to pursue more information from a neurologist in Kansas City. They were able, fairly quickly, to get an appointment with a neurologist at Menorah Medical Center in Overland Park, Kansas, and began making plans to come to Kansas City in the week ahead.

It was another beautiful, blue sky July afternoon when I rode with John and Laura to that first neurologist appointment. Dr. Stephanie Younger had been kind enough to squeeze us into her busy afternoon schedule, knowing the distance they had driven from western Kansas. We were her last appointment for the day. She had already studied the CT scan and was the first to confirm our deepest fears. "I am so sorry, Laura. You have a primary brain tumor. When the tumor appears first in the brain, we note that as a 'primary' brain tumor, as opposed to a tumor which might first appear in another part of the body and later develops cells that migrate to the brain. We could biopsy and determine the grade of the tumor, but it will need to be removed; so really the best course of action is surgery." With that, the words were spoken—a tumor—in the brain. Brain surgery would be needed.

Our minds were reeling as we drove home, too stunned to comprehend what it all might mean. I remember calling Laura's dad and her brothers and asking them to meet us at the house as soon as they could. We all felt as if our "perfect world" was falling apart, especially Laura and John's. I had known others who had battled brain tumors, and knew the prognosis was not good. *How could this be happening to our Laura?* We gathered at our house, cried together, prayed together, and knew God's grace would cover us all as we walked through the days ahead. It did.

Decisions had to be made and so, as we all do, we launched into the "prepare for battle" mentality. We read everything we could find, searched the Internet for clues, researched childhood experiences, talked to those who could offer guidance, re-examined childhood experiences looking for answers, considered all that she had done/not done in her life that might have given us insights, read some more, and then were too frightened to read any further. The American Brain Tumor Association helped us to understand how rare this was for a female of her age and also offered a possible life expectancy of five to ten years after diagnosis. On paper the prognosis did not look good. So we stopped reading and simply prayed. We knew and never doubted our God was able to eradicate any tumors that the doctors might find and that he was fully capable of completely healing Laura if he should choose to do so. Laura never doubted that. Laura also never really questioned, "Why me?" She did not—we did not—spend a lot of time dwelling on the answer to that question. It was what it was, and to spend useless energy pondering that question seemed senseless. Besides, we knew God was able to deliver her, so we simply waited for his timing and watched for his presence.

Her first craniotomy was scheduled for late July at Research Medical Center in Kansas City, Missouri. Dr. Younger had given us the name of one of her associates, Dr. Geoffrey Blatt, a neurosurgeon who practiced at both

Menorah and Research Medical Center. Laura and John had debated over where to proceed since I also had a cousin, Dr. Barry Pollard, who had an excellent reputation as a neurosurgeon in northern Oklahoma, with patients who came from far and near to seek his wisdom and level of expertise. They sought a second opinion from Dr. Pollard, and he was so very kind to offer her immediate access to his operating rooms and his very busy schedule. Still Laura and John sensed that this would become a long, ongoing process, and the thought of being able to rest and recover in our home in the Kansas City area surrounded by people who loved her here had a greater appeal. We trusted God to go before us, and he did, opening Dr. Blatt's schedule so that her surgery could be done quickly under his skilled and capable hands. Many would wait many weeks for a surgery of this magnitude to be planned and scheduled, but Laura was on her way to surgery a mere two weeks after the first seizure. God had indeed gone before us and opened doors, one after another. We learned the importance of knowing and recognizing the people God had placed in our paths over the last year. The CEO of Menorah Medical Center, Steve Wilkinson, had been on staff at St. Catherine's Hospital in Garden City, Kansas, years before and had grown close to John's family. And so there he was, just when Laura needed him, to go before us and "open doors." We saw so clearly more of God's careful orchestration and preparation.

I'll never forget that first appointment with Dr. Blatt. We sat in the waiting room together—Laura, John, her dad, and I. The waiting room was filled with people who suffered from serious neurological problems, some with walkers and canes because of their inability to walk unassisted. Most were quite elderly. It was very humbling to see your beautiful, blonde-haired, blue-eyed, twenty-three-year-old daughter sitting among these patients. She immediately caught the attention of Dr. Blatt's staff with her long blonde hair and short denim skirt. And they also quickly recognized her beautiful heart. She shared her symptoms with Dr. Blatt—the headaches, the seizure, the now constant pressure on her brain. But the CT and MRI clearly showed him all that he needed to know. John and Laura went back alone for the examination with Dr. Blatt, and then Joe and I were invited into his office for his recommendations. I had told Joe as we drove to this appointment that our role as parents would be to now take a step back. The decisions that would need to be made would be Laura and John's. They could seek our prayers and our advice—and they would—but the decision would in the end be theirs. That would be a pivotal moment for Joe and me as we "let go" again of this young woman who had been our little girl. The doctor's recommendation was communicated quickly: surgery, a craniotomy, or resection would need to be done. Then Dr. Blatt carefully and thoughtfully selected his words as he walked us through the years ahead, noting that there would probably be several months of chemotherapy to begin with, and then slowly cautioned Laura and John about having children even if they were able to do so. "I would hate, five years from now, to be sitting across from you, John and Laura, with let's say 'five' children now, and have to communicate even more harsh news to you. Consider carefully how to move forward in starting a family." Those words caused us all to pause.

The day of surgery, July 26, 2000, went well. Laura's dad

led us in prayer very early that morning, pleading for God's protection, for the surgeon's careful hands, and for Laura's life. We stood around our little kitchen table, the same table where we had shared so many family meals, before we made the drive across town to the hospital. It was pitch black when we left home, and the sun had still not risen when we arrived at the hospital. Our pastor friend, Donnie Simpson, met us at the hospital and prayed with us all after Laura's brothers, Matt and Thomas, had arrived. We watched throughout the day as God continued to remind us not to be afraid. Nearly forty-five friends gathered in the hospital waiting room that day to wait with us. This was one of our first "cloud of witnesses." It was at this time God also began painting a picture for me of the church, the true Church, at work. I had known these facts in my brain for years, but now this reality resonated in my heart as well. Those who were encouragers wrote notes of encouragement; the prayer warriors prayed; those with the gift of administration organized the food that was brought and the care that was offered; those with the gift of mercy came and sat and listened. One amazing friend, Syd Gilliland, and her family in the weeks ahead brought us an entire Thanksgiving dinner in 100 degree August heat, which included turkey, pumpkin pie, mashed potatoes, and all the trimmings simply because we had "so much for which to be thankful." I marveled at this realization that the church was not the building; it was the people—all the people— who surrounded us daily with their love.

Sadly, on that same day, we watched across the way as someone from Joe's office also waited for a family member who was having surgery. This individual waited all alone for words regarding her mother. I remember thinking in my mind, *Some of our crowd of witnesses needs to become one of her cloud of witnesses!* That moment profoundly changed my future visits to hospital waiting rooms. In the future, I would remember it was not so much what you had to say but simply "being there" that was important and that no one should sit alone in a hospital waiting room for life-threatening news.

We waited together all through that long morning until we finally saw Dr. Blatt's face coming toward us in his surgical garb. He spoke to John and me, but a crowd of forty-five gathered closely around. "Surgery went well. The tumor seems to be mostly benign." The crowd of witnesses cheered, offered praises to God, and then disbanded quickly to move on to the other aspects of their lives as John and I and Laura's immediate family sat and looked at each other and thought, *Mostly benign? What did that mean?* We knew all too well that even one small aggressive cancer cell embedded in the innermost parts of her brain was not good. We would again carefully wait on God's direction and his timing. Words were already being spoken regarding the long days of recovery ahead, the weeks of chemotherapy to follow, and the next appointments with the neurosurgeon; all we could focus upon was that she was fine.

The days in the hospital passed quickly, remarkably so for brain surgery. I remember slipping into see Laura in the ICU, and all she wanted was to be able to slip into some of her own clothes. John entertained us in the hospital room, trying out all the equipment as only John would do, trying to help the long hours of recovery pass more quickly. She had been placed in a room on the orthopedic floor so the room furnishings included bars and pulleys that were intriguing to John. Friends of ours arrived to visit Laura but could not remember her (fairly new) married name. They simply told the clerk at the front desk, "Pick out the longest name on the list!" knowing that Kleysteuber had to be the right choice, and it was. An African American nurse's aide helped Laura wash her hair and shower for the first time after surgery. Laura and I laughed because this young woman questioned Laura about her symptoms and surgery, wanting to know all she had experienced. She said she had been having awful headaches and just wondered if *she* might have a tumor! Then I watched as my little girl with the brain tumor ministered to this frightened young woman in the shower.

And so we remember those early days, those first days of "battle." We remember the days before and the days after, and most of all we remember this beautiful woman with the gorgeous smile who continued to amaze us all. We had to remember.

To do anything less would deny what God had already done.

Personal Reflection

In what "early days" do you find yourself? The early days of divorce? The early days of a life-altering illness? The early days of joblessness? The sweet, sleepless, early days of parenthood? The early days of becoming a teenager? The early days of aging parents? The early days of rebellion? The early days of great success? The early days of an empty nest?

_____

_____

_____

Will you choose to remember how God is at work during the early days of the story of your life? Are you watching for evidence of his hand?

_____

_____

_____

God never gives strength for tomorrow or for the next hour, but only for the strain of the minute.[6]

—Oswald Chambers

Trust Occurs Moment by Moment

"Trust in the Lord with all your heart and lean not on your own understanding; in all your ways acknowledge Him, and He will make your paths straight" (Proverbs 3:4–6, NASB).

"Commit your way to the Lord. Trust also in Him, and He will direct your path" (Psalm 37:5, NASB).

Colin and Cooper have learned so much about *trust* in these last two years. They have both learned to trust that their bicycles will still hold them securely, even without training wheels. Colin has learned to trust that he can make it through the night without a bottle at bedtime; he has also learned that life is good even without two pacifiers in his hands. Cooper has learned that he can sleep without his favorite blanket or his yellow pillow. They have also learned to trust that Daddy always comes home and that Aunt Jennifer will always be there in the mornings and that Nana comes back and that Papa and Grandma Jan are never far away. Most of all, they are also learning to trust that God will surround them with people who love them even though there is no "mommy" in their lives.

Perfect trust: "The secret to perfect trust is acceptance … acceptance is taking from God's hand absolutely anything He gives, looking into His face in trust and thanksgiving, knowing that the confinement of the hedge we're in is good and for His glory."[7] That is the definition Chuck Swindoll offers in his book entitled *Perfect Trust*, and that is the book my dear friend, Rhonda Allen, gave me that day in July, 2000, when Laura had her first craniotomy. Rhonda tucked it inside a beautiful wood and metal basket that I still have today and also included a tempting arrangement of fruit, yogurt, and muffins. It was so very like Rhonda to offer food for both the body and the spirit. The book's cover shows the simple image of an open hand with a small bird sitting right in the middle of the palm. Perfect trust. For our good and for his glory. I pondered deep in the nights how cancer could possibly be for our or for Laura's *good*, and also how God might use this cancer for his glory. We knew we were about to learn an incredible lesson on trust. It would be a test of how deep our faith truly was. We also had to learn to trust moment by moment. We could not live in the worries of tomorrow; we had to rest in the hope and the trust of today. We knew how faithful God had been for our yesterdays, and we simply had to trust he would also be faithful for the tomorrows.

Laura recovered at our home—her childhood home—during that first week after surgery. She spent many long afternoons on the sofa in our family room, greeting friends from college and childhood friends whom she had not seen for some time. Strangely, coincidentally, it was also during this time that another dear friend of ours passed away. Laura's brother, Matt, had shared a long friendship with Donny Cosse. Donny had married in July of 1996 a beautiful young woman named Amy. The two of them had been overseas serving as Youth with a Mission missionaries in Amsterdam and India. When they returned home in 1999, they learned that Amy's skin cancer (which she had developed as a teenager) had returned and metastasized into lung cancer. The cancer had been growing and advancing during all those months they were overseas sharing the good news of Jesus Christ. She died on August 1, 2000, just days after Laura was released from the hospital. Laura attended Amy's funeral on August 4, along with our family. She would not have missed that opportunity to be fully present for Donny and his family, for Amy, and for her brother Matt. Laura was so very brave as she sat there in her adorable hat, which she wore to cover the surgical scars; we could not imagine what it must have felt like for her to observe the funeral of a young woman just her age when she herself was now facing such life-threatening challenges.

Remarkably, it was also at this very time that Laura's best friend, Vicki, was giving birth to her second daughter, whom she named Lauren. Lauren was born on August 5—Laura's birthday—just days after Laura had had her craniotomy. Laura sent baby Lauren and Vicki a beautiful bouquet of pink roses to welcome her arrival on earth. I marvel now at all that God was carefully orchestrating...Laura's surgery, Amy's entrance into heaven, and Lauren's arrival on earth all in the span of a week. Donny and his family had to "let go" of a precious life, just as Vicki and her husband were welcoming a beautiful new life into their home.

In my position as children's minister at our church at that time, I often had the opportunity to remind parents that one of their hardest lessons in life would be learning to "let go." We bring our tiny babies home from the hospital and the rest of life, all of life, is composed of seasons of letting go—allowing our child to take their first steps, allowing them to leave our arms and be held by the arms of another, allowing them to cross the street for the first time, allowing them to drive a car, allowing them to spend the night at a friend's house, watching as they head off to college and eventually walk down the aisle to begin a new life with someone else. The sooner we learn not to hold on too tightly to the things of this world, the better off we will be. And so it had been for us with Laura. I know that is why Chuck Swindoll[8] had used that *open hand* to illustrate his definition of "perfect trust." God asks, "Do you really trust me? Then open your hands!" It is also only with open hands that we can receive the additional blessings that God has in store for us. We had learned early to "let go," especially with Laura, because her life had been unique from the very beginning.

I believe Laura would want you to know that her life was a testimony of the many miracles that God had performed in her life, but it is really a story for us all. His miracles are all around us if we will simply open our eyes to see them. We often become so very busy with the things of this life that we simply forget to recognize his hand.

From the moment of conception, Laura's life was a miracle. She was born on August 5, 1976—not a pregnancy that Joe and I had planned. She was a "surprise" blessing. I would not have planned to have a second child when Matthew was only eight months old, but she was born nine months later. It was not our timing, but God's. When I learned I was pregnant, I cried. I was teaching school; we had moved back to Oklahoma. Joe was in graduate school after three years in the Air Force, and when I learned I was at a higher risk for miscarriage because of medical challenges I faced at the moment, I cried even more. And then a peace came knowing that God was very much in control.

She was born absolutely perfect with only one small challenge. Her right foot had been tucked up beside her left ear in those last, long months of my pregnancy, so that each time they pulled her leg down it would spring right back up to the left shoulder. Again, we simply wrapped her tightly, prayed for God to relax all those little muscles, and knew even then he was preparing her to dance through life, and she did. We believed that God had designed her and each of our children on purpose for a purpose, and began to watch and wonder how God would use her to impact the lives of others.

She loved playing with her baby dolls, Cabbage Patch doll, and grew to love Barbie and Ken as well. She learned to play the piano, had a beautiful voice, held wonderful carnivals in the backyard, and enjoyed basement adventures with her brothers. I like to tell her two little boys that their mommy and uncles were the early version of the *Backyardigans!* (a favorite show for Colin and Cooper) because of the adventures that they shared. She enjoyed the magic of tea parties, and skating parties, and dance recitals, and hosted mini Olympics in the backyard where she was always the star gymnast. She enjoyed her time with her cousins at family camp and learned to ride her favorite pink bicycle with the then-popular banana seat. Summer days in Lenexa, Kansas, were wonderful. It was also at this point in her life that she met Vicki Garrett. They became best friends, and it became a friendship that would last a lifetime.

Vicki and Laura met at church when they were eight-years-old. They never attended the same school and did not live extremely close to one another, but they shared sleepovers and camp experiences and many afternoons together in our homes. Joe and I, and Vicki's parents too, simply wanted to encourage this precious friendship between two little girls whose families shared the same beliefs and goals and morals. Most of all, both families wanted their children to know that God had a plan for their lives and to know with certainty where they would spend eternity.

Laura was blessed with a rich foundation of faith through years of Sunday School and Vacation Bible Schools and choirs and youth activities, but that did not ensure her eternity. She carried her little Children's Living Bible with her every Sunday to church, along with her pennies and quarters for her offering, but that did not ensure her eternity. Laura was blessed with parents and grandparents who had pursued a relationship with God throughout their lives, but that also did not ensure her eternity. She knew a personal invitation had been extended to her by the God of the universe through the death of his one and only Son, Jesus, and she accepted that invitation to know him and to live for him at the tender age of nine. She certainly did not understand at the age of nine all that this commitment would mean, but she trusted that God would continue to make that clear through all the moments of her life. She also knew that accepting that invitation gave her a "ticket" to heaven, which she would use someday. Someday far, far away.

She moved quickly through the awkward middle school years and entered high school one year behind her older brother, Matthew, and four years ahead of younger brother, Thomas. The word in the hallways at the high school her freshman year was "Have you seen Matt Badgett's sister, Laura? Wow!"

It is not surprising that Laura danced for the drill team at Shawnee Mission West High School or that she was nominated for homecoming queen her senior year, but what I have thought of so much in these last days was how much she enjoyed running track. She had never run in an actual meet before but was anxious to try. Before her very first race for Shawnee Mission West High School her freshman year, Laura asked her older brother, Matt, to take her to the track and teach her how to use the starting blocks. She was nervous about her first track meet and wanted to be sure that she at least started correctly. Matt had already found great success on the track field, and she knew he would teach her well. He did.

She was amazing to watch on the track field with those beautiful long legs and graceful body. She was made to dance and to run. The three-hundred-meter hurdles were her specialty, combining her skill for speed with her love of dance, and she was so very easy to locate on the track field with that long, blonde hair flowing behind her. And especially easy when she ran in Wyandotte County, where she was often the only blonde-haired runner on the field. I thought of all those races she ran as I drove home from the hospital late one night. God knew even then that those last days would be her toughest race of all and that there would be some enormous hurdles for her to overcome. She always ran with such great strength and beauty and perseverance, and that is how she still ran at the end of her life.

As we sent her off to Kansas State University to attend college, we never dreamed that she would fall in love with a farmer/rancher, but indeed she did. We had always prayed that each of our children might know with certainty who they were to marry, and that was very much evident with Laura. I remember clearly when we first began hearing about this young man whom she had met while working together on a homecoming project in the fall of 1996 with her Chi Omega sorority and his fraternity connections. She told me John Kleysteuber was just a little older than she was but a semester behind her in college because he had been "red-shirted" in kindergarten. I loved that fact and embraced his humor from that first moment. Having taught preschoolers for years, I knew the importance of giving our little ones an extra year to grow and develop, just as the football coaches did.

At first glance, she thought he was a freshman and did not want to pursue a conversation until he assured her he was not. Laura also could not believe that John was a farmer and thought for sure that he was simply trying to tease her. He was dressed very nicely in his polo shirt and had a very GQ look about him. She was expecting the farmers at K State to be wearing overalls. She was so very wrong. John had grown up the youngest of five children with four older sisters. They had carefully taught him how to shop and to dress well. He did then; he still does today. One month after she and John met, she was off for her first visit to western Kansas, and I knew then this was indeed "the one." I cautioned Laura about driving that great distance to stay with someone's family whom she barely even knew, but she was determined to do so. John was attracted to Laura's great beauty and her incredible smile and her love of life; Laura was drawn to his good looks, his self-assuredness, and most of all his sense of humor. They danced that evening on their first date, and he made her laugh. She could tell he worked hard, both at "work" and at play. They went on a ski trip together early in their relationship, and she specifically told me about the long conversation they had on that drive home about their faith. Her beliefs were shared by him and that enriched the love that was already growing between them.

They were officially engaged in December of 1997, and were married on August 7, 1998, at Emmanuel Baptist Church in Overland Park, Kansas, in a beautiful ceremony attended by so many friends from far and near. They stood before that incredible crowd of people and pledged to stand beside each other through all that lay ahead, even if it might mean days of sickness or health or days that might be better or worse. From the first day of their marriage until the very last, I know that John would have always said, "The heart of her husband trusts in her" (Proverbs 31:11, NASB), and I know that Laura would have said the very same words about her husband.

Laura asked her younger brother, Thomas, to sing at their wedding. He did an incredible job of presenting the beautiful music and lyrics of Steven Curtis Chapman's song, "I Will Be Here,"[9] and those words later became so very prophetic.

> Tomorrow morning if you should rise, and the sun does not appear; I will be here. If in the dark we lose sight of love, hold my hand and have no fear, 'cause I, I will be here when the laughter turns to cryin' and the future is unclear, I will be here.

Laura and John simply loved the words; they had no idea, no way of knowing, how true those words would become in their lives. Those words, sung by Thomas, were the only moments in the ceremony that brought Laura to tears. They were one of the first of their friends to marry, so it was an enormous celebration of the love that God had allowed them to discover. When we were looking for the perfect place for the reception, Laura made it clear she and her friends wanted to dance. The location had to have enough room to comfortably entertain their nearly four hundred guests, but it also had to have a big dance floor. We searched until we found one that could accommodate this request, and then we danced.

They both completed their final semesters at Kansas State University and then made the move to western Kansas. She embraced her new life in Garden City and quickly began falling in love with the people and her family there. She had grown into a young woman of such beauty and grace that people were drawn to her. Heads would turn when she walked into a room, and then as they grew close, they would recognize her inner beauty as well. She loved all the new friendships God brought to her there. She made the transition from city girl to "western Kansas" girl very easily, learned to Internet shop, and planned frequent trips to Kansas City. She and John dreamed of one day building their dream house with a huge wraparound front porch. Although she enjoyed her career in marketing and her position as marketing director at the Golden Plains Credit Union, all she ever really wanted to do was be a wife to John, a loving mother, a caring friend to those she loved so dearly, a precious daughter, and an amazing sister.

Laura had trusted God with her eternity; she had now trusted him as she made this important life decision regarding who she should marry, and she trusted that a life in western Kansas was the one he had ordained for her. (As long as she could return to Kansas City frequently!) John and Laura were blessed to enjoy almost two years of early marriage happiness before that first seizure led them to the neurosurgeon's office. She had trusted that the surgery to remove her tumor would go well. Now she would trust him with her life.

Six weeks after Laura's craniotomy, we sat in the office of the oncologist Dr. David Lee of the Olathe Medical Center, waiting for him to review her MRIs and pathology reports. Dr. Lee personally invited us back into his office, examined Laura briefly, and then sat down in a chair just beside her. He pulled his chair close to her so that their knees were almost touching, looked directly into the enormous blue eyes of this beautiful young woman, and said, "Laura, I have a four-year-old daughter at home with blonde hair and blue eyes named Lauren. I cannot imagine anyone ever having to say to her what I must now say to you. You have brain cancer."

Silence fell upon us all. No one had used the C-word with us before. This was not simply a tumor that could be dissected, fully and completely removed, cut out with deep margins to spare—but cancer … of the brain. "Also, Laura, I cannot promise you will ever be able to have children. The chemotherapy you will have to take may also interfere with your ability to bear children." Dr. Lee paused for a moment and then said, "I am thankful that you already know the God who is the author of all life." His words of encouragement to us were further affirmation that God was still in control; we could still trust him. I knew God had a dream, a plan, and a purpose for Laura's life. I began to wonder and question how these latest words could still fit into his plans. In the weeks ahead, I would read Louie Giglio's comments that our lives are not truly "our story" but "the story of God"[10] and that this moment we are living now is simply the part where we "come in," where we enter into God's story.

Mary Graham,[11] one of the very gifted Women of Faith speakers, was in Russia as a young missionary nearly thirty years ago. Because of the impact of the Communist government at that time, they were advised not to suggest to the Russian people that God might have a "plan" for their lives but that God had a "dream" for their lives. As she was sharing the idea of this "dream" with one young Russian woman, the young, bewildered girl said to Mary, "Is this true? God has a dream for my life? Does he know that I am a Soviet citizen?"

I paused as I read those words and wrote in the margin of my book, "God, I know you have a dream for Laura's life. God, do you remember Laura has brain cancer?"

In my work as a children's ministry director, I had often

spent summers at camp, enjoying the beauty of the outdoors with seventy-five to one hundred children. A favorite activity at our Tall Oaks Camp experience was the challenge course. The trained leaders would always begin by teaching the children the importance of teamwork in successfully maneuvering the challenges ahead. They began with a series of "trust" activities and the statements and responses were always, "Trusting?" followed by "Trust on!" I cannot tell you how often those words rang in my ears. *Sandy? Are you trusting me?* and my response, *Trust on!* Perfect trust, perfectly offered. Faithful yesterday, just as he had been throughout the stories of the Old Testament, he would be faithful today.

It was not easy. I faltered daily. I doubted; I shed tears; I cried out my heart to God daily. But the next moment would come and I would choose, again, to trust. And that is how faith is built: daily, moment by moment, with each breath that we take, trusting. I also was so very aware of the host of people who were praying us through each day. When I had no strength at all, and when my trust faltered, their faith carried me. Jan Karon quotes Oswald Chambers in her book, *Patches of Godlight*, and perhaps his words say it best, "God never gives strength for tomorrow or for the next hour, but only for the strain of the minute."[12] I had trusted him for today; I could trust him for tomorrow as well.

Personal Reflections

Have you learned to trust perfectly? In what areas of your life do you need to "let go" and simply trust? Are you willing to do so?

_____

_____

_____

Are you able to know with confidence that because he was faithful yesterday that you can count on him to be faithful today?

_____

_____

_____

Thoughtfully consider a challenge you are facing today. How might God use that for good and for his glory?

_____

_____

_____

If you are succeeding without suffering, it is because others before you have suffered

—Adoniram Judson

Suffering and Success

"My comfort in my suffering is this: your promise preserves my life" (Psalm 119:50, NIV).

"Not only so, but we also rejoice in our sufferings, because we know that suffering produces perseverance; perseverance, character; and character, hope" (Romans 5:3, NIV).

Laura's boys were only two and four when she died, so they have had much to absorb and process in their little minds over these last years. I was with Colin one day in the summer of 2008, when he asked me, "Nana, why did my mommy have to have a brain tumor? Why did God make her brain that way?" and then he stopped and added, "She should'a taken all her medicine." In his little world, he had been told so many times if he took all of his medicine, he would get better. So why didn't that work for mommy? One thing I have learned after many years of grownup life is that suffering and success go hand in hand.

My friend and fellow staff member Kendall Lucas was the first to share with me these words of wisdom spoken by Adoniram Judson:[13] "If you are succeeding without suffering, it is because others before you have suffered. And if you are suffering without succeeding, it is so that others after you might succeed." Judson had been a missionary to Burma for nearly forty years in the early 1800s and knew so clearly the link between times of suffering and moments of success. I knew this to be true in my own life as well, but now I would watch as this truth was told in the life of my daughter. This proved to be a season of success for her. I like to call it the "life is good" moment.

Laura recovered from her first craniotomy and then looked ahead to a season of chemotherapy. She was so very optimistic about life, even in spite of her diagnosis, and was confident that God held her future closely in his hands. She was anxious to begin the chemo and to have it behind her so she could get on with life! Laura and John returned home to Garden City. She returned to work at the Golden Plains Credit Union and John returned to his life and work on the farm. Laura planned her chemo treatments for the end of the week at the St. Catherine Cancer Center, so that she could have the weekend to recover, and she did. She learned to deal with the episodes of vomiting and diarrhea, and took long naps on the weekend in order to allow her body to heal.

Laura sent me a beautiful card after she returned home. Our phone calls were becoming more frequent, and it was after one of those late night calls that she wrote, "I saw this card and my heart melted." The front of the card showed a little girl hugging her teddy bear with the words, "There's just no substitute for you!" And then Laura's words continued, "I know this past month has been crazy for all of us. I am just so thankful to have such a loving and caring mother who is willing to do anything for me. It has meant so much during this time. I really enjoyed our long talk the other night. It felt like you were reading my mind. It's just hard sometimes because John does not always understand the emotional side of how I am feeling. Thank you so much for everything you do for me. I love you with all my heart." Her words were simply the heart cries of a young woman newly married, facing such very serious health challenges, and she knew her mom would understand.

Once the chemotherapy treatments began, the doctors cautioned her to be prepared for significant hair loss so we scheduled a day to rendezvous in Wichita for a time of "wig shopping." She had been warned that the loss would happen very quickly, so their recommendation was to be prepared ... buy a wig. That was a heartbreaker of a day for me. Laura had beautiful hair—long, thick, and blonde. She had already trimmed about six inches off in anticipation of losing more of her hair, but the thought of losing it all was more than we could imagine. This had been a concern even before the brain surgery, but the nurses in Dr. Blatt's office had been so kind and considerate and only shaved what was absolutely necessary for the surgery to occur.

John came with us to wig shop, and we mapped out several stores in the area to visit. There were many moments in that long day that were sad, but also moments that were almost comical. The first shop had only wigs that our great-great-grandmothers might have worn; the next shop carried only toupees, and the next very large shop had a myriad of wig presentations (dusty, old boxes stacked floor to ceiling). The sales clerk tucked one long, curly blonde wig upon Laura's head and then stepped back to allow us all a moment to look. John and I had to be careful not to laugh out loud. Laura, with this wig on her head, closely resembled an eighties version of Malibu Barbie, and then we realized that the sales clerk was wearing the exact same wig!

We had to look for moments to laugh, and Laura did as well. We finally found a lovely salon on the west side of town that suggested we might consider ordering a beautiful, synthetic wig, and this is in fact exactly what she did—a beautiful, shoulder-length wig that so perfectly matched her own hair. (John would later wear it to many costume parties.) God was gracious, however, and she did not need it at that moment as she sailed through those early months of chemo with beauty and grace, her ever present smile, and all of her hair.

Oddly enough, providentially so, when I was probably about nine years old, I watched one episode of *Dr. Kildaire* on television in which brain surgery was performed on a female patient and all of her hair was shaved as they prepared to actually drill a hole into her head. It is the only time I can remember as a child experiencing a nightmare that awakened me in my sleep and forced my mother to sleep with me throughout the long night. I had filed that deep within my own brain and recalled it as Laura went through surgery, faced chemo, and shopped for wigs.

Laura was scheduled for regular CT scans and MRIs and always had those documents forwarded to her doctors in Kansas City. It was also at this point in the journey that Laura and John flew to Houston and to the MD Anderson Cancer Center. Years earlier, I had had a family in my ministry with a young father who was struggling with testicular cancer (he even had a western Kansas connection, having lived for a time in Scott City, just north of Garden City). They had made frequent trips to MD Anderson, and their little four-year-old once asked his mommy if these were the "sick people" for whom they often prayed. "Yes," she said, "these are the sick people, and Daddy is one too." And now Laura had joined their ranks.

It was on one of these visits to MD Anderson that a physician asked John, "How many months of therapy did Laura have to endure?"

John paused for a moment and then replied, "None." That was the wrong answer in this physician's eyes. He believed that if you sliced deeper you removed more of the cancer but you also risked altering the quality of your life. Laura's own physician's approach was to be less invasive with his initial "cuts" knowing that you could always return and slice more later. She and John were facing "quality vs. quantity" of life decisions at the tender age of twenty-four.

While MD Anderson has proven to be an excellent answer for treatment and surgery for so many cancer patients, that was not the case for Laura. Her MRIs were misplaced, she did not receive the phone calls to answer her many questions, pathology slides were not delivered to the right locations—the sheer distance alone caused many challenges, and they made the decision to proceed with the plan that her Garden City oncologists and her Kansas City neurosurgeon had outlined. We also believed it was simply God's way of directing us to the people and the care that would be the perfect match for Laura's needs.

MRIs, brain scans, CTs, chemotherapy, craniotomies—we knew already that Laura was standing firm on the many, many years of research and development that had already been done in the area of brain tumors. A very dear friend of mine who had also served as my Administrative Assistant, Celeste Reid, had shared with me the tragic story of the death of her first husband from brain cancer nearly fifteen years earlier. Her husband, Doug Mossberger, had been one of the first one hundred patients to receive an MRI of the brain at Mayo Clinic. The first one hundred patients. How I marveled at that fact. Something that had become so commonplace had once been so rare. Laura would stand strong on the knowledge gained from Doug's illness. She would stand strong and find success because of his suffering. And in time, others would stand strong and find success because of Laura's "suffering." I also stood strong on the knowledge and insight that my friend Celeste had learned from her experience with Doug. And I often bombarded her with questions. I prayed someday I would be able to offer someone else the strength and encouragement to ease the suffering they might be bearing. Suffering and success; success and suffering. God knew exactly what Celeste had endured and purposed for her to be by my side when all this was about to happen to me and to our Laura. Suffering and success; success and suffering. Those words of Adoniram Judson apply to every aspect of our lives, not simply our health. I have reflected on those words even in regard to my years of ministry and my years as a mother and my years as a human being. God positions people in our lives as lifelines of hope and strength and encouragement, just when we need a strong hand to hold us. Suffering and success; success and suffering.

In the fall of 2001, Laura and John came to Kansas City for a visit. I will never forget Laura standing at our kitchen table in her light blue overalls announcing, "I'm pregnant! We're going to have a baby!" Amazing. God's provision was already such an enormous answer to prayer. It reminded me of the moment in the *Father of the Bride* movie when the young woman announced, "I'm getting married!" only Laura's words were, "I'm having a baby!"

When she was almost seven months pregnant, she came to Kansas City for her dad's twenty-fifth anniversary celebration with Hallmark Cards, and at the same time I slipped into a new ministry position at another large church in our area; but we all knew, and told our employers and friends, the world would soon come to a momentary stop when our first grandchild was born. Especially with what Laura had already endured, we had to cherish the beauty of the moment that was about to unfold and honor what God had done. Their first son, Cooper Harold Kleysteuber, was born on March 28, 2002. Visits with the neurologist and neurosurgeon continued, but life was indeed good. New baby, new house, and she and John had carefully planned so that she was now able to stay at home with her precious new baby boy. She adored being a mother. She was just one of those women who so beautifully and instinctively knew what to do with this most precious gift from heaven. She loved nursing her babies, adored bath and nap time, play time, time with friends, bedtime stories, good-night prayers, and hugs and kisses. She was very content at this season of her life to be able to stay at home with her baby boy; her life was busy and full and blessed. She knew when she held her little Cooper that she held a little bit of heaven in her arms.

In February of 2004, she announced that a second little one was on the way with an anticipated arrival date of late August 2004. We could not help but remember those early words that were spoken by each of her doctors, "You may never be able to bear children," but we also knew that God clearly knew the deepest desires of Laura's heart. She and John also chose not to know the sex of their children in advance. They knew that God was carefully designing exactly what they needed and cherished the surprise element of that moment.

I will never forget the drive to Garden City on September 1, 2004. Laura's dad and I drove west to welcome their second child into the world. It was another of those perfectly, blue sky days we often experience in Kansas. We were about an hour away from the hospital when God began painting this beautiful image in my mind. I watched as he began drawing to the windows of heaven all the people who had been so significant in Laura's and John's lives who had already gone ahead of them into heaven. There were her grandparents, her nana and papa, John's grandfather, and other loved ones that they both knew—all being encouraged to find a place next to the window of heaven so they might experience this little one's arrival on earth. It was also then that I was reminded of the two moments in life when the world should come to a complete and utter *stop*. One is when we are "welcoming babies" into the world, and the other is when we are saying our last good-byes. We would later determine that it was at this very moment, the moment of my "dream," that Colin Joe Kleysteuber arrived on earth.

Laura loved this season of life: new babies, playgroups in the neighborhood, afternoons enjoying the light-hearted episodes of *Oprah* (her *Favorite Things* show and her *Road Trip with Gayle*), evenings of laughter with John while they watched old episodes of *Jerry Seinfeld,* Sundays at church, K-State football games, Rice Krispie treats shared with friends, bouquets of pink Gerbera daisies on her kitchen table, episodes of *Grey's Anatomy,* shopping for the newest fashion for herself and clothes for the boys, and decorating their little yellow house on Andover Street. John worked long hours on the farm and Laura learned to adjust to his very busy schedule. She purposed to keep the boys up later at night, so that John could spend precious moments with them at the end of his day.

I was reminded again of the cycle of suffering and success; days of healing after her surgery, challenging days of chemo, but also days of such great, great joy with the births of two precious little boys; and for the moment, her treatments seemed to be guarding the tumor well. The challenges and unknown future with a brain tumor were daunting, but we also marveled at the remarkable ability surgeons now had to take pictures inside your brain and to have sophisticated imagery that allowed them to slice deep into the brain without harming vital sections. The past suffering of so many thousands of patients was now allowing Laura to stand strong and to find success. And some day the suffering that Laura had endured would allow others to stand strong. We were so very thankful.

Personal Reflections

On whose suffering have you been able to stand strong, and in what areas of your life has this been true? Who will stand on your suffering?

_____

_____

_____

Are you willing to "count it all joy," believing that it will be ultimately for good and for God's glory?

_____

_____

_____

Think about how these words relate to your success in work, in life, in ministry, and in your family. On whose suffering do you stand?

_____

_____

_____

What will you do with your blue sky day?

Arise, Stand Upon Your Feet

"But rise and stand on your feet; for I have appeared to you for this purpose, to make you a minister and a witness both of the things which you have seen and of the things which I will yet reveal to you" (Acts 26:16, NKJV).

"Before you throw back the covers, and your feet touch the floor; ask God to show you what he has in store; for the day that's just starting, from beginning to end; God says he'll be near you, if you trust in him." So begins a little children's book about a little elephant entitled, *Dear God, It's Me*[14] by Lynn Hodges and Sue Buchanan that I enjoyed reading to Cooper. I was not moved to tears easily, but on this night for those moments, I was rendered speechless as tears flowed. That little elephant reminded me of an important truth that I would cherish through the years ahead, to remember to always pray before my feet touched the floor each morning, and to also pray before I tucked them in bed each night. As we closed the last page of that book and then said our prayers, I asked Cooper, "Do you think that is a mommy elephant sleeping with the baby or a daddy?"

"It's his mommy, Nana. I know it is." And that is when I really cried. Each day as I rose from my bed and stood upon my feet, I knew God was going to show me new things and teach me new lessons that I would later testify of. I became a witness of things that I had seen and the things he would yet reveal to me.

In mid-October 2004, just six weeks after baby Colin was born, Laura drove to Kansas City by herself with both little boys tucked in their car seats for her next all-important visit with her neurosurgeon, Dr. Geoffrey Blatt. They had continued to communicate with each other through each of the years; her sharing any concerns that she might have had, and him carefully reviewing each of her MRIs. At that time, Laura was still hand carrying the several-inch stack of MRIs that she had collected through the years. She brought them to each of her appointments with Dr. Blatt to carefully review.

The morning of her appointment, she came downstairs to our kitchen very early with tears in her eyes and simply said, "Mom, I'm so very scared. John and I have looked at the MRIs, and we know there have been some significant changes." They were not trained physicians, but they had also looked at all her slides so often through the years that even their untrained eyes could see differences in the images. We clung to each other briefly, prayed, and then got the boys and ourselves ready for the morning ahead. We had arranged for Cooper to play with a friend and baby Colin came with us.

Laura did not have to wait long; Dr. Blatt invited her back to his office. I went with her, and he very quickly affirmed what Laura already feared: there was new growth in the tumor, more which needed to be dissected, removed, and analyzed. I was standing behind Laura, listening, and holding little Colin while fighting tears myself. It was at this point that Colin began to cry; it brings tears to my eyes even now. I wonder did he sense, even then, how very drastically his little world was about to change. His screaming became so loud and mournful that I knew Laura could not hear a word that Dr. Blatt was saying, so I slipped out to complete an all-important diaper change. Once that was completed and Colin was re-bundled, his fears calmed and his tears ceased. I came back into the examining room just as Dr. Blatt told Laura she would have to stop nursing. It was at that point Laura began to cry. She had held herself together as he had talked to her about the tumor and the ramifications of the new growth, but the knowledge she could no longer nurse her baby boy broke her heart.

A second craniotomy was scheduled for November of 2004. This time the surgery would be done at Menorah Medical Center, a beautiful facility near our home with a host of physicians, and nurses, and administrators with whom we had now become familiar. As she had done with her first surgery, she had to go to the hospital the day before the surgery so that the "positioning points" for the intricate mapping system for the surgery could be placed on her skull. She came home looking like someone had glued white life-savers to her forehead and skull. Cooper thought that was, as his daddy would often say, "Hilarious!" and requested he have stickers added to his head as well.

The four hour surgery went well, but it was a long day for us all—especially Laura. Friends came and went throughout the day offering their concern, their prayers, and their support; it was once again the church at work. Our pastor friend, Donnie Simpson, once again came and simply sat and waited and listened. They tucked Laura into a bed in the ICU for the night, and all but John went home to offer our prayers of thanksgiving for her life and for what lay ahead. I slipped into her room very early the next morning to check on her as the nurse was very kindly and tenderly trying to untangle the bloody mass of hair at the back of Laura's head. Dr. Blatt would later tell us that the new formation had been very vascular in formation; therefore, there had been an unusual amount of bleeding. It would be days before that mass of hair was washed and brushed and combed.

She was visited by a myriad of friends and family members, and I brought baby Colin to the hospital each day to sleep beside her. Although he was only six weeks old, he was born weighing over eight pounds. We always said he was very sturdy, and his little body did not seem to mind the changes in his little diet. After recovering from her surgery, their little family of four was anxious to get back home to western Kansas and headed that way as soon as Laura was able to travel. After a brief respite in Garden City, Laura returned to Kansas City for a visit with the oncologist, Dr. Lee, whom she had first seen in 2000. He agreed with Dr. Blatt's assessment that it was now time to become more aggressive with the treatments as we attempted to ensure that no new growth would occur. She could live with "containment" if that could successfully be accomplished. Dr. Lee also made a very significant suggestion. He listened to some of the frustrations that Laura had following her visits to MD Anderson, and he suggested that she might consider the Brain Tumor Center at Duke University (the Preston Robert Tisch Brain Tumor Center) in Raleigh-Durham, North Carolina. That brought a small glimmer of joy to Laura's heart because her very best friend in all the world, Vicki Garrett Harmon, now lived in North Carolina, only a few hours away from Raleigh. Dr. Lee said that he had really been impressed with the level of personal care and attention that his Duke patients had received. It would be an easy approach to have the world-renowned physicians at Duke coordinate and guide the physicians in Garden City with only a few trips to the Brain Tumor Center scheduled each year. For a seriously ill young woman living in western Kansas, this was an excellent plan.

Their first visit to Duke was scheduled soon after that. The trip was amazing. Not only did they meet with an entire team of doctors (with reputations known all over the world), who would oversee her case, they also met a host of others, including a social worker who even made the suggestion that they apply for disability for Laura and their sons. Her cancer had "disabled" her from overseeing the books and accounts for the farm and the ranch so this information became a true answer to prayer in the days and months ahead and still is even today. They did a biopsy of the tumor on this first initial visit to Duke in order to determine the grade of the cancer. John commented later how very much they missed having their friends and family near as they waited alone for the doctor's words. He and Laura both missed the cloud of witnesses that always gathered around them in Kansas City or in Garden City. Waiting alone was indeed so very lonely.

Not only were the medical aspects of this trip so encouraging, the trip also offered Laura great emotional and spiritual strength as well. Her dear friend Vicki drove to Raleigh to meet them, and after Laura's appointments were done; they shopped, laughed, cried, talked, and prayed together. She, John, and Laura shared a hotel room and began the habit of eating at PF Chang's, a restaurant that they loved in Kansas City, but one which they rarely had an opportunity to visit.

The friendship Laura shared with Vicki was a precious gift from God, a rare and treasured friendship that had begun when they were both only eight years old. They had lived together through braces and bicycle rides, dance lessons, summer camps, boyfriends, first bras, first loves, marriages, new babies, and all the challenges of life. They had never attended school together but had enjoyed so many church activities together—camps and choirs and sleepovers. Remarkably, the movie *Beaches* with Bette Midler and Barbara Hershey came out when these girls were approaching their early teens. I cannot tell you how many times they watched this movie about two best friends together facing one's untimely death. It became so much a part of who they were that Vicki would often sign her notes to Laura "CC" and Laura would sign her letters to Vicki "Hillary." Only God knew how true to life this movie would become for these two young women. Laura had been there for Vicki when her husband suffered a horrific highway accident that resulted in a traumatic brain injury and faced a long recovery, and Vicki now would be there for Laura. They had never lived near one another in their adult life but treasured the time they spent on the phone daily, often several times a day, and knew the special place each one held in the other's heart. We marveled at how God had allowed them to find each other upon this very crowded earth. Vicki would later say these words about her friendship with Laura:

> I was blessed to have one very special friend in my life. One friend who would know every tiny detail about me. The one friend God hand-picked for me before I even knew her. The one who would share my soul with me for twenty-one years. She was my "sister," my confidant, and my secret to getting through life's daily challenges. I take joy in knowing that I will see her one day as we spend eternity together. I am so very thankful for her presence in my life.

That special friendship with Vicki and her presence in North Carolina made all those trips to Duke so much more bearable.

After reviewing Laura's case, the Duke physicians mapped out a detailed plan for the months ahead. Then they issued the chemotherapy orders to the oncology department in Garden City, which then adhered to the Duke recommendations; Laura was using mostly oral chemo drugs at this point, and the long months of winter and summer moved quickly past her. Cooper turned three, and baby Colin turned almost one. For those observing Laura's life from the outside, her life appeared perfect with a beautiful family, beautiful home, and a loving husband who was an incredible provider—lots of reason for hope and joy and laughter. Laura also did a beautiful job masking any physical pain she experienced; she did not want to burden others with conversations of headaches and vomiting, late night insomnia and episodes of shingles, or just the constant pressure in her brain. She was not one to complain. She had now had the tumor within her brain for five years. Others forgot. We never did.

In August of 2005, Laura and John and the boys all came to Kansas City for a Kleysteuber family wedding. Those August days were so hot. Laura had not been feeling her best. She wasn't sure why, but she also knew that she had experienced some tiny lapses in time, moments that would seem to pass without her total awareness. She was mindful of these moments and cautious. This particular Saturday she had loaded the boys in the Suburban and was headed to the Plaza area to pick up John, who had spent the night with his family on the Plaza. When she left the house that morning, she told me she wasn't feeling quite right, but she hoped that she simply needed some food and was planning to stop at McDonald's to get her and the boys a light lunch. You need to know that all through this year of illness, Laura still looked amazing; her tall slender body, her beautiful blonde hair, her gorgeous smile, and engaging personality were still completely intact. Few believed or understood the health challenges that she faced.

She left the house. I remained at home, and the phone call came only moments later. "Mom, I'm feeling really strange." I asked her if she was still driving and was elated to know that she had pulled off the road. I knew the heavy traffic she faced as she drove from our home to the Plaza and did not want her to be disabled in that dense traffic. I asked her if she knew where she was, and she answered very slowly, "I don't know … I'm not sure … my mind is working so slowly." I kept asking her short, brief questions as she answered with short, brief replies. I encouraged her to look around her and to tell me what she saw even as I was slipping behind the steering wheel of my car. She looked and said, "car wash" and then the word, "tile." I knew in that moment the exact intersection—a place where she had frequently washed her car with a tile shop located just across the street. I finally determined that she was not too far from our house in an almost empty parking lot, and I raced to find her there.

When I arrived at the intersection of Nieman and Shawnee Mission Parkway, I spotted their black Suburban in the parking lot in front of the tile store. The car was in park with the AC still on when I found her. Laura was nearly slumped over in the seat when I arrived, rubbing the temples of her forehead, trying to ease the pressure and the pain. I attempted to get her to move to the passenger side so that I could drive, but she simply didn't have the strength, mentally or physically, to do so. I hopped into the back seat to check on the boys, and in that moment she experienced a grand-mal seizure. I watched helplessly as violent, involuntary muscle spasms took over her body, as her eyes rolled back into her head, and as she lost consciousness. Her seatbelt held her firmly and safely in place as the spasms ripped through her body. The moments seemed like forever, but truly were less than a few minutes in length. While I knew this was a possibility, it still so surprised me since this was my first time to observe what would transpire during those next long moments. I cried out to God and held tightly to her, all the while also being mindful of her two little ones beside me in the seat. As the seizure subsided, I went into action. Grabbing my phone, I called and left a message for John, dialed 911, and simply prayed all would be well.

An ambulance and two police cars were quick to arrive. They were so very attentive. One immediately moved to assist Laura, and the other came to the back to check on the boys ("Is this little guy supposed to be eating French fries?" There were burgers and fries all over the backseat of the car.) They agreed to move Laura to the ER at Menorah Medical Center so that she could be examined, and I followed in the Suburban with two little guys "racing" the ambulance. Our family was all quick to arrive at the hospital, and the ER staff began assessing Laura's condition and administering fluids. We really didn't think they would keep her in the hospital, but we also were anxious for their assessment.

Late in the afternoon, they sent her home with instructions to check in with her team at Duke on Monday. She came home, rested, showered, and then prepared for her evening ahead. She put on her makeup, fixed her hair, and then slipped into her strapless, hot pink party dress so that they could all attend the gathering that evening. John attended the wedding and then came home to pick up Laura and the boys for the reception. It was a very hot August night. Laura wanted all four of them to go, but she also asked that we stay available to come and "rescue" Colin when he would grow weary in the hours ahead. We had a call about eight thirty in the evening and drove out to meet them at the beautiful country club just west of our home. When we pulled up, we spotted Laura in the hot pink dress seated on the curb with baby Colin pressed to her chest. Her dad snapped a picture to capture the moment. That image, that picture, will forever be a reminder to us all of Laura's faith, her hope, and her endurance as she walked this journey with brain cancer. Her family was so important to her; her faith was so strong, and she knew that God was gently walking beside her throughout each of her days. She continued to do all that she could to enjoy every moment, to be fully present because she knew the uncertainty of her days, and that became a precious gift.

John and I would talk about that "gift" in the days and years ahead. When Laura and John learned of her cancer, they were also given a rare and special gift by the author of all of life. We all tend to put off until tomorrow those things which we long, we dream, we desire to do. Laura and John learned to embrace the moments of today and to not postpone until "tomorrow" the things that were precious to them and to their family.

So on that hot August evening, I arose to my feet, pulled that little baby from her arms, took him home to sleep and to rest, and continue to testify even today of all that I have seen and all that God has done. Twice in five years Laura experienced a seizure while driving her car, but in both instances she was aware enough to know that she needed to pull off the road and seek help. God performed so many miracles in both instances: no one was injured, her body remained free from harm, she didn't injure another party, the car was intact, and the lives of two little babies were spared—all on a blue sky day.

Personal Reflections

Is there an area of your life where God is asking you to "arise and stand upon your feet," when all you want to do is fall flat upon the floor? What have you seen? What have you observed? What have you endured that God is asking you to testify of? Are you willing to do so?

_____

_____

_____

Today, this very day is a gift. What will you do with your blue sky day?

_____

_____

_____

Each moment is a miracle; each day a
new beginning.

We Pour Out
Our Hearts

"Pour out your heart like water in the presence of the Lord. Lift up your hands to Him for the lives of your children" (Lamentations 2:19, NIV).

Imagine what it is like to hear your three-year-old grandson pray that his mommy's brain tumor might be healed by the great and almighty God of the universe. And imagine what it is like to hear that prayer repeated again, again, and again. Laura and John had become very involved in the Bible Christian Church of Garden City and did not doubt that the people of that church and so many others were lifting them daily in prayer. We tried to count once all the churches that had Laura's name on their prayer list but simply could not list them all. We knew that prayers were being offered for her from around the world. A dear friend even submitted her name to the prayer group at Brooklyn Tabernacle Church in Brooklyn, New York. We knew a symphony of prayer warriors surrounded us all. A small church in western Kansas made a lap prayer quilt for her, and it was also about this time that a special group of friends under the leadership of Paige Kraus and Katie Unger began meeting with Laura on Sunday nights. They called it their prayer group. Some of the young women who attended were not even sure of their own faith, and some had never spoken a word of prayer out loud; but as they were watching Laura face all that lay before her, they marveled at her faith and were so very curious. We all seemed to be searching for ways to "pour out our hearts like water before the Lord" for the very life of this daughter, this friend, this wife, this mother, this sister, this child of God, and so these friends gathered every Sunday and prayed, pouring out their hearts.

Laura wanted to stay busy and involved in the lives of others, so she volunteered to serve as director of the Vacation Bible School for the summer of 2006 at her church. Throughout the fall of 2005, she poured her heart into enlisting volunteers, designing sets, creating rotation schedules, and pursuing and understanding the right curriculum to use. She decided upon *Fiesta! Where kids are fired up about Jesus!* a wonderful curriculum designed by GROUP Publishing Company. We all marveled at her strength and her focus and her commitment to fulfill this ministry that she so loved. And at the same time as we watched her struggle with health issues, we reminded her, "You don't have to do this! Anyone would understand if you chose to walk away!" But she did not. She loved giving of herself and allowing her mind and heart to focus on things beyond her brain tumor. Besides, she loved the thought that children in her community might fall head over heels in love with the very same one who was guarding and protecting her life and her care.

In the fall of 2005, after Laura's second major seizure, we began to sense an urgency in her illness that had not been there before. The team of doctors at Duke had decided that the best course of treatment at this point of the journey would be four cycles of oral chemo followed by two months of radiation. They were hoping to shrink the tumor as much as possible and then radiate whatever was left behind. Their ultimate goal was total annihilation of the tumor, but even no new growth would be excellent news in the weeks and months ahead. It was a challenging fall. I began making my first trips out to Garden City to stay a week at a time at the beginning of each new cycle of chemo. I would typically arrive on Sunday, be there for her Monday treatment, and remain through those early most challenging days. My primary goal was to keep the boys busy and happy, while at the same time offering John some time back on the farm and keeping watch over Laura as well. My days were filled with trips to the zoo, bike rides in the neighborhoods, play time at the park, afternoons in the driveway with friends and neighbors, all the while checking in on Laura as she slept and rested. Laura's brother, Matt, joined me on one trip and came with me to pick Laura and John up at the airport in Garden City after one of their trips to Duke. I remember standing in the airport parking lot with Matt and Colin and Cooper as I waited for the passengers to disembark, and out of the corner of my eye I briefly caught a glimpse of this beautiful young woman standing by herself holding what appeared to be an artist's portfolio. I thought briefly, *I wonder what young art student might be flying into Garden City?* Or perhaps, I thought, it was a young woman on a business trip carrying her marketing plans. And then I heard a voice yell, "Mom!" and I looked again and realized that the young woman was my daughter looking so beautiful and so healthy, standing there holding her "portfolio" of MRIs of her brain.

As I was helping Laura with her daily challenges and trying to be so supportive of John and the boys, I was also still working as children's ministry director for a very large vision-driven church in the Kansas City area. I loved the work and the children's ministry team that God had allowed me to gather around me, but I also was very aware of the pace at which this ministry moved forward. I loved being able to go to work each day with the clear knowledge that I was doing important work with an eternal connection, but I also had important work to do in western Kansas. I had for many months been weighing how much longer I could carry on while also being attentive to Laura's needs.

The church was supportive and had been generous with my time away; but still the demands were great, and I placed a very large burden of responsibility and accountability upon myself. Early in January 2006, while actually on a staff retreat, I made the difficult decision to step aside from my ministry position so that I might turn my full attention to Laura and her family. I cannot tell you how hard it was for me to let go, but I also knew absolutely that it was the right decision, the wise choice.

We knew that in late January, Laura and her family would be temporarily moving to our home in Kansas City so that she might begin the two months of radiation that the Duke team was now recommending. When I told Laura of my decision to resign, she sent me the most beautiful bouquet of pink roses, with the following sentiment attached, "Each moment is a miracle; each day a new beginning." She signed it, "To Mom, with much love for your sacrifice, Laura."

On one of my last days of ministry, I walked back to my office with tears in my eyes. I had spent the morning outlining for the new team all that they would need to know for the months ahead. After nearly twenty years of ministry to children, I was entrusting all that I knew to a new younger team of leaders. I was grateful for their willingness and enthusiasm, but it was still hard to let go of this work I had loved and labored for so very much. As I walked to my office that day, our Hispanic custodian, William, happened to see me and noticed the tears in my eyes. He questioned me and then offered to pray for me. I was eager to hear his words offered to our heavenly Father in his Hispanic native tongue. My young assistant, Ashley Stroup, along with William and his wife, gathered with me around the little trash can in my office. There was not a sweeter, tenderer prayer that had ever been offered on my behalf. I will cherish that moment always and will always be grateful for the way in which he shepherded my heart on that day as a pastor should. It was also a very personal reminder that there were many who were daily pouring out their hearts, not only for Laura, but for me and for all of our family.

My last day in ministry was on a Sunday, and Laura and John and two precious little boys arrived only a few hours later. Joe and I had hoped to have a week to rest and refresh, but that was not what God had designed. It had been so difficult for me to step out of the "current" of ministry and watch the flow of the ministry continue past me, but in the weeks ahead I was able to trade my service to over five hundred children to a tiny ministry of two little boys, a beautiful daughter, and the husband who loved her.

Our season of "radiation" began with Laura's pre-radiation appointment on the following Monday with a wonderful Christian radiation-oncologist, Dr. James Coster. While there, the technicians made a "mask" for Laura, which she would then wear during each of her treatments. It was molded to resemble all of her facial features so it then offered the "positioning points" that would be needed for all the intricate mapping to occur during the weeks of treatment ahead. The radiation beams would be directed precisely at those positioning points. The following week, when she began her first treatment, she simply stretched out upon the table and the mask was placed over her face and then screwed into the table. Her head was "locked" into place for the precise location of the area of her brain that needed to be radiated. The session only lasted moments. She received treatments Monday through Friday each week for almost seven weeks. Remarkably, God had given her a peace about this whole procedure. She said that the mask fit so tightly that she really could barely open her eyelids.

She did have some meltdown moments when she realized the full impact of what lay ahead—moments filled with tears and doubts and questions, but overall she remained so very strong. There had been times in my own work in which I had said, "Sometimes the more you know, the more you wish you didn't know." I believe the same applied to Laura. She needed to know and understand all that was happening, but the more she knew the more frightening the future appeared. There was a certain bliss, a certain innocence, in not knowing. The radiation treatment amplified the seriousness of her condition. She sent the words of this e-mail to her friend Paige during those early days of radiation:

> I do have some bad days, but that is true for us all, just in different ways. The first week I was here, I cried myself to sleep every night. One night, I took out my Bible and read until two a.m. The next morning, I felt like a new woman. Even John noticed the change in my spirit. God is watching over me. God is good. I think about you all. Please write, call, e-mail anytime. I would so love to hear from you.
>
> Love, Laura

Looking back now, I had no idea my daughter was crying herself to sleep because I was usually up very late and would arise throughout the night with a one-year-old who could not quite sleep in this bed that was not his own. It was difficult for me to guard both his little heart and hers, but I would have, had I known of all her emotions in the dark of the night.

Her friends in Garden City created a beautiful silver box of wishes/prayers and scripture for Laura to bring with her to Kansas City to help her through those long, long days. I remember her carrying that tiny little box up to her bedroom to place beside her bed when she arrived at my house for the season of radiation. She carried it with such tender care, knowing how precious those words would be in the days ahead. I knew that she read those words daily, and remembered the many friends that were praying her through these long, hard days. John also took precious time off from the farm during this long season. He would come and stay a week, then return to the farm for a few days, and ride the early morning train back to Kansas City. Laura drew such strength and courage from his presence; it was important for him to be by her side.

During this season, I became very disconnected from my previous life, but I also rediscovered story hour at the library, took long walks by the river with my boys, took time to ride bikes, remembered how much fun it was to have art sessions and do puzzles, and quickly remembered what it was like to have a little one sleeping between Joe and me. I also marveled at how God had so carefully orchestrated all of Laura's care and was overwhelmed at the thought of all those who had gone before Laura, whose earlier treatments of brain tumors had now enabled her to receive the very best care possible. Before the invention of the mask for Laura's type of tumor, the physicians would tattoo your face between your eyebrows and your temples; and before that, they used an indigo dye to map out a grid on your face. *Suffering and success.* I continued to praise God for all the thousands of brain tumor patients who had gone before Laura and prayed for all those who would one day follow after her. The team of doctors at Duke had attempted to isolate and hopefully shrink the brain tumor with four cycles of chemotherapy in the fall of 2005. Now they hoped to radiate all that remained and continue with chemo at the same time and would follow with more chemo all summer long.

They also placed her on a heavy dose of steroids in order to reduce the swelling and pressure in her brain; and along with the drugs came distressing side effects which she was forced to endure. The steroids Laura was given were corticosteroids, which are different than the anabolic steroids sometimes used by athletes to build muscle mass. In brain tumor treatment, these steroids are used to ease the accumulation of fluids in the tissue around the brain. But as the steroids work, they also cause you to endure significant weight gain, additional gastro-intestinal challenges, muscle weaknesses, mood swings, insomnia, and—saddest of all—a puffy, "moon-like" face. Laura endured each of these, along with the challenges caused by the chemo drugs.

Laura's appointments were scheduled for 2:50 each day, so our lives revolved around that important session. I wrote in my e-mail that week:

> I was reminded this week that the radiation treatment is a "one-time" opportunity, praying for miraculous results from this aggressive approach to eradicate and eliminate her tumor. With radiation you run the risk of not only damaging cancer cells but "good" brain cells as well. (God, please protect her brain, guard her ability, her love, her desire to continue to be the wife and the mother that she so longs to be.) We are anticipating a summer of

chemo to follow, but that can be done in the comfort and quiet of her own home. Her medications arrive via FedEx mail directly from Duke. I believe the last batch that was dropped off at the door was valued at over nine thousand dollars.

Beth Moore[15] speaks this way about "pouring." She says that we each walk around this earth with our little "cups" asking each other, "What can you pour into my life?" I simply begged for prayers to be poured into my "cup" so that all who knew Laura and our family would pour out their hearts and prayers to the Father on her behalf. At the same time, I knew God alone was the only one who could heal her. I prayed that he would but did not know how he would choose to showcase his glory. I remembered those words by Louie Giglio that reminded me that my life was really not about me; it was all about God and what was best for him to accomplish his purposes and plans on earth. Knowing the severity of Laura's illness did not make that any easier. We poured out our prayers. Laura poured her heart into her *Fiesta! VBS*. I poured out my life into two little boys, and the people of Garden City and our family and friends poured out their prayers on our behalf. None of us knew the enormity of the journey that awaited us.

Personal Reflections

What people have sacrificed and "poured" out their lives on your behalf?

_____

_____

_____

For whom are you "pouring" out your life, your prayers, and your concerns?

_____

_____

_____

What do you need poured into your "cup" today? What do you have to offer to others?

_____

_____

_____

The wait between Good Friday and Easter Sunday...the wait between the promise and the fulfillment.

The Enormity
of the Journey

"Then Jacob made a vow, saying, "If God will be with me and will watch over me on this journey I am taking and will give me food to eat and clothes to wear so that I return safely to my father's house, then the LORD will be my God" (Genesis 12:9, NKJV).

Cooper loves to pack and also to pretend. He doesn't really have to be going anywhere; he simply loves to pack! If he can find a suitcase or a backpack, he will fill it with all the toys and snacks and clothes that he just might need for the journey ahead. In recent months, I have had to tuck all the backpacks on the highest shelves because he will fill them all! When we are looking for a lost item, we have learned to check all the backpacks. He has also already told me that someday he hopes to visit the Great Wall of China, a place two of his heroes, Dora and Diego, have also visited. He has looked at the world globe and knows that this will be a long journey. Both boys are looking forward to going on a real "bear hunt" journey with their daddy in the months ahead (a promise that was made by John when he was coaxing Cooper to ride his bike without training wheels). Perhaps God is teaching him to always be prepared for the journey ahead and that some journeys are not easy.

After the season of radiation, the team at Duke asked Laura to be a part of a clinical trial in hopes of confining her cancer while at the same time gathering important research for the years ahead for other brain-cancer patients. She shared with me the enormous stack of papers which she had been asked to sign in order to become a part of this study. The information was both encouraging and frightening at the same time. She had to carefully initial every page. The content was sobering. The words on the very first page were enough to cause tears to come to my own eyes. *You are being asked to take part in a research study because you have a malignant (cancerous) brain tumor... the drug combination you will be receiving has shown promise in animal testing but very few, if any humans have used this study drug combination... if you agree to take part in this study, there may or may not be direct medical benefit to you. We hope the information learned from this study will benefit other patients with brain cancer in the future.*

She began the new regimen of chemo drugs on April 24 and was told that she would be a part of the trial for as long as perhaps even a year as long as she continued to make progress. She was told that there would be forty individuals with brain cancer in her study. She would be using a combination of drugs which until that time had only been tested on a healthy group of laboratory rats with malignant brain tumors. Her first visit to Duke in April after the radiation offered words of hope: "no new growth." We celebrated that news; it was *good news*, and yet she had already endured nearly five years of treatments and chemo, two months of radiation, and now this clinical trial.

The words in my e-mail that evening expressed my thoughts at the time:

> I think Laura was more prepared for the news this time than I perhaps was. While we are all so very thankful, we all want closure. We all want to know that our prayers have been answered and that we can now move on to the rest of our lives! We want to shut the door on cancer and radiation and chemotherapy and move on. Our prayers have been answered, just not exactly in the way that we would choose. Her battle continues. She has reached the top of yet another hill and now must strap on the "combat boots for cancer" and charge the next hill. She told me last night she was just hoping to rest for a while. We simply will continue to pray that God will use her life as an inspiration to others. It is strange the verses that will come to your mind at times like these, and today's for me was Psalm 20:7: "Some trust in chariots and some in horses; but we trust in the name of the Lord our God" (NIV). Perhaps because in the last days we had talked about all the treatments that are now available and how you

could spend a lifetime researching them all, but in the end we know that God is the Great Physician and that he is the one guiding and directing her care. We rest in that knowledge. We trust his care. We all continue to be so blessed by the tapestry of spiritual gifts that have surrounded us, from friends far and near. We watch as each act of kindness soothes our souls in some small way. And we are grateful.

After the trip to Duke in April, Laura returned home to live life and continue her treatments there. Severe headaches had become part of her daily routine. She had also been on a very high dosage of steroids during the radiation and they wreaked havoc with her already fragile body. The most obvious result was the addition of about forty pounds, and her beautiful face swelled until her eyes receded into all that additional fluid upon her face. Even for me as her mother, it was so hard to watch. I prepared her brothers and her dad so that they would not be shocked when they saw her. She was so very sensitive about this fact. One day in Garden City, she made a stop at a business that she had often frequented. The owner did not recognize her until he saw her name on her check, and then he said, "Wow, you've really gotten big!" She walked out of the store in tears and never returned. John and I were forbidden from ever shopping there. She would pass friends in Target or Wal-Mart and they would pass her by, not recognizing the woman she had become. She understood, but at the same time it broke her heart.

Thankfully, after the Duke assessment, the doctors recommended that she begin weaning herself off the steroids. The negative side effects of the steroids seemed to be outweighing the benefits. It would be a slow process, but she looked forward to regaining some control of her own body. When so many things are out of control in your life, you are anxious and excited for the few things that you can control.

Easter Sunday came and went, and I was encouraged by the message our pastor offered. He talked about the "wait" between Good Friday and Easter Sunday morning, the "wait" between the promise and the fulfillment. I shared in my e-mail that week:

> I find myself at the quiet place between Good Friday and Easter Sunday. We have faced the "Good Friday" moment with Laura as we have accepted the impact of her disease and now cling to his promise for healing. And personally I have faced another "Good Friday" as I have released my hold on my ministry and look forward to what lies ahead for us all and for me personally. I had been reminded earlier last week that sometimes God allows a faith crisis so that he might continue to show us the "good" that he will accomplish through these seemingly desperate situations. We each must live through our own Good Fridays and silent Saturdays in order to arrive at our personal Easter Sundays and see our hopes and dreams resurrected.

I was ready for a personal "resurrection" for us all.

Laura's friends in Garden City sensed the intensity of the journey had heightened, and they searched for ways that they could offer their support: prayers and wonderful meals, cards, letters of encouragements, personal visits, and phone calls were all appreciated so much. Through all those long months of her illness, Laura and family were blessed by so many wonderful meals. Friends and family kept a steady flow of healthy, nourishing meals coming through their doors for so many months. More than even the food, Laura looked forward to visiting with family and friends as they brought those meals to their home. She, who had so often done this for others, was now benefiting from their rich generosity. Friends far away sent gift cards for restaurants and businesses in the area. We all searched for anything to lighten the load that she and John were carrying.

The clinical trial involved a very heavy dose of a new type of chemotherapy, and that began to take a toll on her body, both physically and emotionally. Her blood counts were checked frequently and often fell to levels lower than the doctors would have preferred. They would then delay the next chemo dosage for a few days and then would ask that she go ahead and begin. We believed that they were hesitant to leave her "unprotected" for very long. The white blood cells allowed her to fight infections; the red blood cells carried oxygen throughout her body; the platelets allowed her blood to clot. Keeping these "counts" in the right balance and at the right levels was a daily challenge. The drugs she was taking for the Clinical Trial could throw off the balance of any of these, and yet, without the chemo drugs, the tumor would advance and grow. It was a very delicate, yet critical balance for her medical team to seek to maintain.

May 30, 2006: Laura has begun her clinical trial, and as they had warned her, the sixth, seventh, and eighth day of her first cycle of drugs have hit her very hard. She so wants to be strong and independent but is battling fatigue and nausea and is finding it difficult to manage herself, much less her little guys. I will be leaving again in the morning and will stay at least a week to help her through the most difficult days. Then John and his family will assist her as needed. I always enjoy my days back home with Joe and feel guilty for resting and for feeling "well." I have just continued to pray that she might be blessed with "normal" days and that she would find strength for today and hope for tomorrow. "Do you not know? Have you not heard? The Lord is the everlasting God, the Creator of the ends of the earth. He will not grow tired and weary, and his understanding no one can fathom; He gives strength to the weary and increases the power of the weak…those who hope in the Lord will renew their strength" (Isaiah 40:2–8, NIV). Praying it would be so today and tomorrow for Laura.

I was in Garden City when Laura had the joy of watching over a hundred and fifty children attend their evening VBS, and I watched as she gathered every ounce of strength she had to lead and guide the volunteers and children that week. She had become increasingly aware of how very sick she had become and was also realizing the enormity of the journey that lay ahead.

July 4, 2006: In 2004, when Laura had her first surgery, I was preparing my weekly kids' lesson, this time from Matthew 8:8, the story of the Centurion's faith. The centurion begged Jesus, "Just say the word and my servant [our daughter, John's wife, Cooper and Colin's mommy, Matt and Thomas' sister, our dear friend] will be healed" (NIV). That has continued to be our prayer. We do not doubt God's ability to completely heal her body, but do not know how he will choose to display his power and his glory. Yet we plead for her complete and total healing. God has gathered around her such an "audience" of people who are watching her faith be lived out daily. We ask that you pray today for her immediate well-being, that her fever will disappear, that she will be able to tolerate the new chemo levels as the waves of nausea come, that she will be able to eat so that she may keep all of the medications in her system, and that her spirits will be lifted as she sees God at work; and through it all, that God's healing touch might come.

When I arrived at their house in mid-July 2006, Laura ran out of the house and into the garage, just as I was pulling into the driveway. The boys were napping, and she said, "Mom, I just talked with our pastor, and he said he could see me *now*. I just have to go." And she was off.

These were the days when the full impact of Laura's illness and the enormity of the journey truly came into focus for her. Looking back, I wondered, "How could she have not known how sick she was?" She knew. We all knew. It was just so very hard for any of us to speak the words. And also we held on to so much *hope*. We did not want to believe all that we had read. When first diagnosed in July 2000, we read everything we could find, devouring words on treatments and "cures" and solutions and suggestions, and then we stopped reading (the words were too fearful), wanting to believe that she would instead beat the odds. She was so young, so healthy, and so strong in mind and body, so loved, and her faith—our faith—was so strong. Surely God would hold all of that in her favor? We also sought the best physicians, the most current research, and believed that she did receive the most incredible care available to her. Still it was not enough.

When she had been at Duke only a few days earlier, she had read an article on the Internet that quoted her very own world-renowned doctor stating the percentages and the realities of what she was up against. She gave me only moments to read the words that had so frightened her, and I quickly scribbled some of those words on a tiny pad of paper in my purse:

> Three-fourths of the two thousand patients at Duke are in clinical trials. Although they are making great strides in the treatment of brain tumors, there are still more failures than successes. Brain cancer is almost always fatal. It is the leading cause of cancer deaths with people under the age of thirty-five. In every one hundred patients, only a few live longer than five years. The three-to-five year survival rate is only 18 percent.

Laura had already beaten those odds. Reading those words spoken by her own doctor and quoted on the Internet with such sobering statistics brought her to her knees. They were frightening words for anyone, but especially for a young wife and mother to hear, and were made even more so by the way her body was feeling at the moment. The clinical trial and the new chemo regimen were both wreaking havoc with her now fragile system. She had completed the two months of radiation earlier in 2006, had finally been able to get off the heavy dosages of steroids, and was now carefully adhering to the directions of the team of doctors at Duke. It was all so very hard for her to do and for us to watch.

I stayed with the boys that July afternoon while she met with her pastor. She came home, and although he offered her great empathy and comfort and prayer, he really did not know what to say. How could any of us know what to say? He admitted to feeling inadequate in situations like this and kindly offered her the names of some of the professional counselors in the area. While I was there, and in the weeks ahead, she made several appointments with a licensed counselor, but even those visits were not very helpful. Can anyone really prepare you to face death when you are not even thirty years old? She found herself feeling as if she was counseling the counselor. And so those visits stopped. Perhaps God purposed that to happen so Laura would continue to rely solely upon him.

While at Duke that month, Laura and John carefully purposed and planned for a few extra days on the beach. Even Colin and Cooper were able to make this journey, so Cooper had a chance to pack his suitcase. After their days at Duke, they relaxed with friends Vicki and Tommy at their home in North Carolina for a few days and then traveled to the ocean for some quiet days of family time. Laura loved to photograph family moments, and she loved the ocean and the beach. She returned home with beautiful images of them at the beach, pictures of the boys' names scrawled in the beach, pictures of them all standing on the dock and romping in the ocean waves. She had begun to lose her hair, and it had thinned considerably. She had been warned that this loss would be permanent, but even more sobering was the news from Duke that the tumor had grown.

On July 21, I wrote in an e-mail:

I just had a call from Laura. They were enjoying the ocean waves off the coast of North Carolina and then were headed to a new aquarium to see the "sharks and the porpoises!"

She and John were at Duke yesterday for the two-month assessment and did not receive good news. The tumor had grown, not much, but any growth is not good. Based on that, and the fact that she had not tolerated the meds well, they are removing her from the clinical trial. Her team of doctors is recommending a more aggressive approach, one they typically take with a Grade IV tumor. Her last biopsy, several months ago, still indicated that hers was a Grade III. They are not sure that hers has indeed "upgraded" but believe this even more aggressive approach is necessary.

When they return to western Kansas this week, she will begin a new chemo treatment, taken intravenously for four hours once every two weeks. Each cycle will be six weeks long, and she will continue this approach for a year. She will continue her trips to Duke at approximately three-month intervals. Although this treatment is new to her, it is not considered a clinical trial. Her blood counts have dropped "dangerously low" in these last weeks, although she has felt better than she had for months! Their family was all here with us Tuesday night and she looked amazing. You would never know by simply looking at her the battle that rages within her body.

We know and believe God continues to orchestrate her care and simply covet your continued prayers for her physical and emotional well-being and for a complete healing. Remember also John and Cooper and Colin. Strength for today, hope for tomorrow.

The enormity of the journey again stretched before her.

Personal Reflection

How do your words ease the burden or add to the burden someone else is carrying? How have your words helped or hindered another's journey?

_____

_____

_____

Who has added weight to the enormity of your journey? What words of encouragement have you offered today?

_____

_____

_____

What words of encouragement do you need today?

_____

_____

_____

Your prayers lay down the track on which God's power can come.

—Watchman Nee

New Growth/ Growing in Faith

"My health may fail, and my spirit may grow weak, but God remains the strength of my heart" (Psalm 73:26, NLT).

For Christmas 2006, I purchased a growth chart for Colin and Cooper. I was so proud of myself for making my selection early at one of my favorite "Nana" stores and for then having it personalized: The Kleysteuber Boys, Colin and Cooper. It even came with small places for pictures of the boys, individually and together. After they had opened the gift, I helped the boys take their shoes off and stand straight and tall against the wall so we could mark how tall they were. We laughed because Colin has inherited his mother's height and his daddy's build. He is very sturdy. Cooper has inherited his mommy's build and his daddy's height, thus they are almost the same size! We love to see how tall they have grown, and it always reminds me of the pencil marks my own daddy kept on our many walls. In fact, that's how one of Nicole Nordeman's beautiful songs, "I AM"[16] begins: "Pencil marks on the wall, was I always this tall?" As parents we are so very careful to monitor our children's growth patterns. I only wish that didn't also apply to brain tumors.

Growth—new growth—is wonderful news when it is spoken in reference to the tender, small plants you have planted in the ground, or when your young child is making those ever-frequent visits to the pediatrician's office. Growth is desired in the life of a church and is longed for when you have watched a new love blossom. Growth is especially good news when it reflects news of maturity in the life of your teenager, and there are times when we, as women (and maybe even men), long for our hair and our nails to grow. But the words "new growth" has a very fearful sound when they are made in reference to your daughter's brain tumor. It is especially disheartening when you have spent six years, immeasurable amounts of money, nearly all of your options, pursued treatments all over the nation, and it is spoken in reference to your beautiful only daughter's brain tumor. Laura never heard the words, "We got it all." She never heard, "Clear, clean margins." She was thankful to hear "stable" and loved the words "no new growth."

When we received those words "new growth" in late July, the decision was made to remove Laura from the clinical trial and pursue a more aggressive chemotherapy. Also during this time, they made the difficult decision to surgically place a port, or point of entry, for her next series of chemo. There was a debate about even this decision because this new drug would cause her body to have difficulty in healing itself, thus they had already cautioned her about any cuts or bruises or abrasions. They were not anxious for a surgical procedure, even a very small one. However, the oncologist was also fearful of injecting the chemo directly into her veins because he knew how caustic the drug would be. Basically, they would be injecting her with "poison" in an attempt to rid the body of the cancer. This newest chemo had proven to be very successful in the treatment of colon cancer, but it was very experimental in the treatment of brain cancer. Plus she would be given double the dosage that was normally given to an adult for colon cancer. *Double the dosage.* She experienced extreme nausea, exhaustion, weakness, and so much more, but that did not begin to cover the assault on her mind and heart.

A favorite quote for me had become the following words by Watchman Nee:[17] "Your prayers lay down the track on which God's power can come. Like a mighty locomotive, his power is irresistible, and always available, but it cannot reach us without the rails." Friends prayed daily for her strength and that her hope would also stay strong. We needed that power to come upon us with the force of a locomotive. Any one of us could tolerate the pain and agony for a brief time if you have the confidence that it will pass and that you will have some "good days" before you begin again. That was our daily prayer. She had completed only one treatment and had twenty-five more to go in this next phase of her cancer battle. We did not doubt that her care was being orchestrated by God, directed by the Brain Tumor Center at Duke, and administered by the oncology department at the Cancer Center in Garden City. Friends and family prayed, the port was inserted without extreme difficulty, and she was ready to begin the next treatment.

A sweet friend, Katie Unger, gave her a Bebo Norman CD the night before she began her newest chemo series and asked that she listen carefully to the words of "Borrow Mine":[18] "Take my hand and walk with me awhile, 'cause it seems your smile has left you. Don't give in when you fall apart, when your hope is gone, you can borrow mine; when you can't go on, when your faith is hard to find, you can borrow mine." Laura's faith had not left her, nor had she lost all hope, but it was so comforting to know when you are so very weak you have the strong shoulders of others upon which you can lean.

On August 5, 2006, Laura turned thirty years old. Any other year it would have been a wonderful celebration. If together, I would have baked her favorite strawberry cake, and we would have enjoyed a family dinner together. We would have gone shopping for a few new things (clothes!) for her and retold again the story of her birth (a favorite thing for her mother to do for her children on their birthdays!), and we would have looked back at pictures from her childhood. If we had not been together, I would have mailed her our usual "birthday in a box" surprise for those times when distance kept us apart, and her husband's family would have organized a birthday lunch with all of his family. We knew the importance of celebrating the life of each individual on their special day.

But on this birthday, Laura was in the midst of yet another serious cycle of chemotherapy to combat the brain cancer that had invaded her body. I had been in their home in western Kansas for another week of intense chemo. We did share some presents, but she really wasn't strong enough for the cake and celebration. Her presents from her dad and me were unusual yet just what she needed: a new set of eight-hundred-thread-count sheets in a very pale "butter" color to match the new comforter she had just purchased (she was spending so many hours in bed and needed that softness next to her body), two plastic white trash cans (one for her bedside and one to keep near the sofa, for the many times throughout the day when she was compelled to vomit), her soft "lamby" blanket from our house (her favorite blanket "throw" that she loved to snuggle in when she was back home), and a beautiful wall plaque with the simple word *hope* etched on the front (I carefully added the Scripture verse from Hebrews 11:1 on the back).

We all offered unusual gifts this year on her birthday. Her husband, John, planted a tree in the backyard to honor her; a sweet thought—a loving thought—but not exactly what she needed on this day. I believe John had hoped she might see the tree as a symbol of hope and life; but for Laura, he may as well have offered her a kitchen appliance. On this day, she didn't need a tree, or a shrub, or a new mixer; she needed a gift straight from his heart. So he quickly went into the bedroom and offered her a second gift which he had already purchased for their anniversary which was only days away—a beautiful new diamond wedding set, beautiful and breathtaking. Laura had endured so many months when she was unable to even slide her rings onto her finger because of the swelling from the steroids. This was a beautiful gift, an extravagant gift from a husband who wanted to shower his wife with reminders of the beauty and great love she had brought to his life, not knowing how brief that life might be.

In spite of our feeble attempts on this birthday to honor her, we all knew the one gift we so longed to offer but could not ... and that was the gift of her health. Only God could determine if that gift would arrive, beautifully wrapped. Still she knew how very much she was loved and how hard each one of us was praying that she might regain her strength and her health.

My e-mail on August 13 shared these words with family and friends:

> We continue to be so very thankful for your thoughts of encouragement and for your prayers. Laura has done remarkably well these last few days. So well, in fact, that she managed to catch a ride to K City to crash at our house for a few days and enjoy time with family here. That, in itself, was answered prayer. (It would also be the last time she was at our house, although we did not know that at the time.) John did not get to come but has had four long days back home on the farm playing a catch-up game of his own. I will be driving Laura and the boys home on Sunday, so covet your prayers as we travel.
>
> Laura begins her second round of the new chemo regimen on Monday at ten thirty. As we have said before, if she can have the hope of a few "good days" in between the so very challenging days of sickness, she will persevere through the long year ahead. She has great determination and faith. I have treasured the words from a Beth Moore Bible

study that I did earlier this year: "If anything is too hard for you right now, then you have the perfect setting for a miracle."

How I prayed that might be true and then closed with this verse:

> Therefore, we do not lose heart! Though outwardly we are wasting away, yet inwardly we are being renewed day by day... so we fix our eyes not on what is seen, but on what is not seen. For what is seen is temporary, but what is unseen is eternal.
>
> 2 Corinthians 4:16–18, NIV

During these days little Cooper was really captivated by the adventures of *Dora the Explorer* on television and especially delighted in helping her find which path she should take. I prayed each day that when he was a little older he might understand the importance of seeking God's direction and path as he launched out into this big, wide world. We knew and believed God had so carefully directed Laura's path and had led her to an incredible team of doctors who were intent on eradicating this dreaded disease. A friend also reminded me that very week she had no doubt that God would heal Laura but that he must still have a number of people he desired to draw unto himself and Laura yet had a role to play in that. Until then, we would continue to pour out our hearts like water before the Lord. We prayed for significant growth in our own spiritual lives and that more and more might be drawn to a faith in God because of Laura's faith. Kingdom growth, a prayer that we knew God would indeed honor.

Personal Reflections

Is there something in your life right now that is simply "too hard" for you? Are you watching, then, for your "miracle"?

_____

_____

_____

How have the challenges in your own life helped your faith to grow? Do you pray for a challenge-free life for your children or that they might grow deep roots through the adversities of life?

_____

_____

_____

Bring a smile to God's face by what you do today.

—Max Lucado

Being Fully Present

"There is a time for everything and a season for every activity under heaven" (Ecclesiastes 3:1, NIV).

Be fully present in this moment.

Laura and her little boys became accustomed to having someone always present with them, whether it was Daddy or Aunt Jennifer or Nana or Grandma Jan or a friend. Laura had very little energy for herself, much less an active four-year-old and a busy almost two-year-old. But she also wanted to be as "fully present" as she could be, interacting with the boys and giving them her early-morning kisses and late-night hugs. She would ride with John to drop off Cooper at preschool on the days that she felt well enough, simply because she was able to do so. She would enjoy an early-morning game with the boys on the sofa and snuggle with them in her bed after afternoon naps. And when the sun was shining, she would join us on the front porch for a while or sit in the backyard and watch the boys play in the sandbox.

On one particular Friday, as I was leaving to return to Kansas City for a few days, Colin and Laura were both sleeping, and Cooper was watching a movie as I slipped out the door knowing Daddy was on his way home. Colin woke up with questions, "Nana? Where is she?" as he looked downstairs to "my" room. Cooper told him very matter-of-factly, "Colin, she's gone. She'll be back in *one* day" (that's a week to him). Colin immediately threw himself on the floor and began crying. It was nice to know that my presence would be missed and that they would look forward to my return.

My weeks in Garden City were long. We all missed our lives. We missed what our lives used to be, but we were all also adjusting to the "new" normal. God continued to show us joy and laughter in each new day, and we were thankful for that. One night at dinner, Cooper simply began singing the words to the children's song "This Little Light of Mine" on perfect pitch. (He had learned it at school that day and simply wanted to share it.) We marveled at his ability to remember the words and the tune as he offered this precious gift to his mommy. And Colin would run to grab a hat each time we would leave the house to take mommy to get her shots or to have her blood drawn. He knew his mommy was wearing hats (to cover her hair loss), so Colin thought he surely must need one as well. God sprinkled our days with these wonderful moments of joy and laughter, laughter and joy, and enabled us to have the strength to move forward. Cooper would ask each of us at the dinner table each night, "So what was your favorite part of today?" We looked forward to all the responses. We treasured those moments around the dinner table and continue that practice still today. I kept my bag of clothes always packed for these weeks away; the basic items that I needed for a week of caregiving. I just marveled at the preparation God had given me even for this! The years that I had done children's ministry camps and family camps and even my father's own military background. I would sleep on a cot (trundle bed) at Laura's; rise at dawn and make sure all the lights were out at ten; serve as night watchman, cook, cleaner, and camp nurse; read stories; plan games and crafts; provide shuttle service; keep everything on schedule; and follow the orders I was given. It sure sounded like camp or the military to me!

As I drove across Kansas for my next stay at Laura's, I would often reflect on the plight of the early pioneers as I drove over and through the western plains under that bright, blue sky. I was so thankful for the car that I drove to protect me from the elements and to allow me to arrive in just a little over six hours. I considered the long, long journey that our forefathers had made and marveled at their courage and their bravery and their fortitude. It was also in the quiet of my car that my tears would so often flow. I would offer those last hugs and kisses (so hard to let go and leave), peel little arms off of my body, step into my car, and the downpour of tears would begin. I would often attempt to call Joe as I was leaving town, but as soon as I heard his voice, I would be so overcome with emotion that I would be unable to speak a word. As I drove, I listened to music to encourage my heart and allowed the tears to simply flow.

We celebrated Colin's happy birthday number two on September 1, with a big party and lots of family, even though this was not one of Laura's "good days." We had a chocolate "barnyard" cake with lots of cows on top, balloons, and presents for her little boy to enjoy. He received some incredible toys and a toddler vehicle that came fully equipped with tools for the road. Laura was so thankful to be able to enjoy the day. She said to me many times that week, "This is my life now; I will not be robbed of the moments that are important to me." She was so determined to be fully present, especially for John and Colin and Cooper.

In mid-September, Joe and I traveled to Big Cedar Lodge in Branson, Missouri, for a brief, private respite for the two of us, while Laura traveled to Denver, Colorado, for a Women of Faith gathering with her friend Paige. She was a little nervous about being away from her doctors but also was so excited and anxious to spend this special time with a close friend. Paige had given her the tickets for this event as a gift for her birthday in August. Before leaving home, Laura carefully packed a "medical folder" for Paige with all the most current information on the prescription drugs she was taking and all the contact phone numbers for her various doctors. They spent a wonderful three days listening to inspirational speakers; hearing powerful, uplifting music; staying up late to talk; eating out; and even took time to buy a beautiful Pottery Barn comforter to cover her little one's soon-to-be-big-boy bed.

It was also at this Conference that Laura actually recorded, in her journal, some of her very last written words.

She was blessed to hear Max Lucado[19] speak, and this is what she heard him say:

> You have only one shot to shine.
> You can do something that no one else can do!
> Everything, everything is for God's glory.
> Bring a smile to God's face by what you do today.
> —*Thoughts shared by Max Lucado*

I have often wondered what she must have felt, hearing those words and reflecting upon them with the future of her life now hanging in the balance. It was so much to be considered by one so very young. The days she was now living were truly her "one shot to shine."

In my journal on September 16, I wrote,

> I am home again from western Kansas. Laura has completed four treatments, eight weeks, twenty-two treatments to go, forty-four weeks, and then our "one year" will be over. The weeks continue much the same with my arrival on Sunday night and chemo on Monday. She continues to battle extreme nausea and fatigue during those initial days and then will finally have a few "good" days before she faces the challenges of the treatment again. She has lost most of her hair and continues to lose weight. Sleeping pills and anti-anxiety drugs help her rest throughout the night and day. She keeps her plastic trash can right beside her bed and another right beside the sofa so she never has to take a step when the meager contents of her stomach are ready to spew from her fragile body. Even with all of this, her spirits remain

good, and she is constantly encouraged by the words and calls from family and friends and packs so much "living" into the few good days that she has. We have learned the importance of the word *stable*, and simply hearing those words at her next Duke appointment would be so very good and an answered prayer.

Music had always spoken to my heart, and I recently heard it said that music "softens the soil of your heart." I love that because there are so many songs that have so touched my heart in recent days. Music speaks to our souls in ways that mere words simply cannot. One of those songs has been Chris Rice's song, "Untitled" (Come to Jesus).[20] Our niece, Jennifer, recently sang this song so beautifully at the memorial service for Joe's father. The first lines begin, "Weak and wounded sinner, lost and left to die, O raise your head for Love is passing by. Come to Jesus, come to Jesus, come to Jesus and live." Each time I hear this, I think of the John 5:2 reference of the sick and infirmed that would lie beside the Pool at Bethseda, waiting for a healing touch from the Savior; and then I think of Laura as she lies on her sofa or bed, barely able to lift her head, knowing that all she has to do is keep her eyes focused on the God who loves her, who is also the Great Physician. She is. We are. We appreciate your support and prayers so much.

The date on my e-mail said October 4, 2006. I had been in western Kansas for eleven days. My usual trips lasted five to seven days. It was easiest for me to arrive on a Sunday evening, enjoy the week with my little ones, assist Laura as much as I could, and try to shift some of the daily challenges from John's shoulders to mine. When Laura was feeling reasonably well, my presence allowed John to get back out to the farm, which was important to him on so many levels. He felt so guilty for not being fully present on the farm, especially during this fall season, and he also needed the brief mental and emotional relief of focusing on something other than how very ill his wife was.

I had arrived the Sunday before, and Laura had had a reasonably good week. We had enjoyed our usual days of morning trips to the Cancer Center for blood-level checks, taking Cooper to preschool while Laura rested and then afternoon naps for us all. I usually planned at least one brief outing with the boys each day just to get them out of the house to run while a friend stayed with Laura. The park, the amazing Garden City Zoo, the pet store, and the play land at McDonald's were some of our favorite stops. On the days when Laura needed to have blood drawn, we would drive slowly to town. The sudden twists and turns of the roads could send Laura's head reeling, so she always asked me to take the roads cautiously. It even seemed strange to drive, for she loved to do so. As we approached the Cancer Center, I would pull right up to the front doors so the boys could watch while she was inside. The weather was beautiful; so I could roll the windows down, and Cooper would shout, "Be brave, Mommy! Don't cry! And remember to push that little button to open the door! (The handicap button on the main door to the center.)" Off she would go, and we would sit and watch for her wave from inside. Those days changed late in the week. Laura suffered a mild seizure late Thursday evening after going to bed and then a grand-mal seizure very early Friday morning. John was with her both times. I was sleeping in my trundle bed down the hall, "guarding" the little boys throughout the night so that Laura could have an undisturbed night of sleep. This was John's first time to witness one of Laura's seizures. After the second seizure, John took her to the ER at St. Catherine's. The day began there, and then they finally admitted her while a CT scan, MRI, and EEG were all completed. We waited over a very long weekend for the Brain Tumor Center at Duke to receive and review all of the data that was sent to them. They shared the news with John late Tuesday afternoon. There had been more "new growth" in the same area that had shown new growth over the summer while she was still on the clinical trial. The bottom line was that the current regimen of chemotherapy was not working, not being effective, and was not powerful enough to slow the growth of this now very invasive cancer. The physicians and cancer team at Duke recommended more chemo, simply a new and different combination, with the recommendation for that new cycle to begin the following Monday. The appointment that had been scheduled for Duke for later in October was postponed until November. They were anxious for her to complete two cycles of the new chemo regimen before returning to see them. I wonder now if they knew then or if they doubted that she would make it that long.

That hospital stay, over that long weekend in October, resurrects so many memories. The weather was beautiful; how we wished we could have been outdoors enjoying the sunshine and blue sky. Laura was confined to a floor with many elderly patients just down the hall from the pediatric ward. One of those afternoons, the nurses allowed John and me to stay in the room while they performed an EEG on

Laura. A strobe light was used to seek to induce a seizure, and they were successful in doing so. The nurses began by asking her a series of questions. Simple questions that on any other day she would have known the answers to so very easily: what is your name, where do you live, what is your favorite color, when is your birthday? We waited and held our breath while she struggled to pull each small piece of information from her mind, knowing her ability to do so would be so vital to her well-being. She knew she lived in Garden City and knew that her favorite color was pink and remembered her name but couldn't recall the answer to the last question. As we watched, we could simply imagine the synapses in her brain struggling to retrieve each small piece of information but knew that the cancer was also blocking her ability to retrieve the information that she needed. This time the seizures had impacted her ability to fully reason, to comprehend, to communicate what her heart and mind wanted so deeply to say.

So many friends came to visit at the hospital. They would sit and try to have conversation with Laura; and sometimes she made perfect sense, and other times it was clear that she was not thinking correctly. When Katie stopped by, Laura handed a bottle of hand cream to one of the nurses and then whispered to Katie that it was actually "cocaine." Strange words that she had heard on the news and from life were being twisted and turned in her mind to appear to be reality. Even she knew they were not correct; still, that was what came out of her mouth.

One day as I left the hospital briefly to grab something for dinner, I happened upon Katie and Laura's friend Paige in the parking lot. They were sitting there, on the curb, in the bright sunshine, preparing to pray together for Laura. Their small prayer group was still faithfully meeting, and when Laura's condition had grown worse, they were anxious to lift her name to her heavenly Father. They asked me if I would like to join them, and it was my joy to do so. What else could we do, and yet that was the most important thing to do. I paused and watched and listened and knew God was seeing great spiritual growth occurring in the lives of these young women.

We began to pray that the new chemo combination would be less debilitating and yet more effective than the last had been. Laura was weary; worn out, confused, and still struggling with the headaches that were a constant part of her life. The seizures had really taken a toll on her both physically and mentally. She left the hospital with a feeling of "disorientation" and some short-term memory loss. We continued to pray that her ability to think might return to normal as the anti-seizure drugs took effect in the weeks ahead.

On October 20, Laura took time to carefully write a "last letter" to John and tucked it safely in a drawer for him to find after she was gone. She would later not even be able to remember that she had done so. In that letter, she told him, "I don't know what God's plans are for me ... but I think I have accepted in my heart, and my head, that my life on earth will probably not last very much longer. I am not scared. It only makes me so sad to think about not being with you or the boys ... thank you for filling my heart with love and laughter ... and *no regrets*."

I think of that now and marvel at her ability to say so.

She began using strange words for common everyday

things. The word *tortilla* became one of her favorite words, and she even used it when she asked us to lock "tortilla"— the front door.

Her balance became unstable, and she fell more than once when she would forget how unsteady she had become. She fell once down a short flight of stairs, screaming all the while, "I'm okay!" and then, took a hard, frightening fall into the corner of the brick fireplace, hitting her head and side of her body. That fall evoked a mournful scream that scared us all. I was sure we would be headed to the ER for stitches, but she did not even bleed. She was protected in ways we could not even imagine while remaining determined to continue to function as she normally had.

On October 22, 2006, I noted in my email:

> I head back to western Kansas this afternoon. Laura has continued to feel about the same, minor seizures throughout this past week, but nothing that has stopped her completely. She and John and the boys decided at the last minute to head to the Broadmoor Hotel in Colorado Springs just for the weekend. Cooper was really looking forward to swimming in the indoor pool. They need time as a family in a fun environment, especially on those few days when she is feeling better. Chemo treatment will begin again on Monday at ten thirty followed by the oral chemo she is taking each day. We are simply praying that it will be less challenging for her but more effective than any of the other treatments have been. My car is packed with pumpkins for the boys, surprises for Laura, food for the journey, frozen casseroles for her freezer, and a vast array of fall and winter clothes

for whatever the weather may bring. We are praying for beautiful fall days to enjoy.

There are so many who now have their eyes and their hearts focused on Laura's story. We are praying that God will use this as an incredible opportunity for us all to proclaim, just as Elijah and the people did in 1 Kings 18:39 when they cried out "The Lord, He is God! The Lord, He is God!" (NIV). We pray that God might use this moment of Laura's story to showcase his glory in miraculous ways that testify of his strength and power.

They had a wonderful time at the Broadmoor and in Colorado that week, making family memories that they would never forget. They took walks around the lake, went swimming in the pool, and picnicked on the floor of their beautiful room that evening. The next day they enjoyed Imagination Station at the Focus on the Family headquarters, visited a dinosaur museum, and had dinner with friends. Laura had usually been the photographer in the family, but on this occasion John carried the camera and was mindful to take a precious picture of Laura walking on the grounds of the Broadmoor with Cooper and Colin each clinging to one of her legs. As we later looked at that photo, we marveled at how each of their steps were perfectly in sync with one another.... each had his left foot up and right foot down; and as the boys held so tightly to her legs, Laura's eyes stayed focused on the road ahead. That has become a favorite picture for us all that so beautifully captures this one moment in time that they shared.

As I left town that week, I reminded Laura that God could just as easily use this new form of treatment to heal

Sandy Badgett

her as he might have used the last and that continued to be our prayer. We did not doubt that he was able. Just as Laura so wanted to be "fully present" in the moment, God was also always fully present in the moments of her life.

Personal Reflections

Are you living in your yesterdays and longing for your tomorrows, missing the beauty of your todays?

_____

_____

_____

If you knew that today would be your last day, how would you then live?

_____

_____

_____

What would you write in a last letter to a loved one?

_____

_____

_____

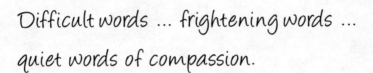

Difficult words ... frightening words ...
quiet words of compassion.

The Power
of Words

"At one time, all the people of the world spoke the same language and used the same words" (Genesis 11:1, NLT).

"And when Abraham's servants heard their words, he bowed himself to the ground before the Lord" (Genesis 24:52, NASB).

"Now you shall speak to him, and put the words in his mouth and I will be with your mouth and with his mouth, and I will teach you what you shall do" (Exodus 4:14–16, NKJV).

Words…the ability to effectively communicate what our hearts and minds need to say. Some can easily share words of great joy but are rendered speechless when they know the sadness their words will bring. And some do not care what impact their words will have. The words simply spill forth from their mouths and make us wonder if they had any idea how painful their words would be for us to receive. Others are gifted in tenderly and gently sharing difficult words, words that will bring great sadness or words that will forever change the course of our life. Wouldn't it be amazing if God would simply put his "words into our mouths" and teach us what we should say and do? He will. We simply forget to ask him to do so.

I have been deeply touched in this last year by small words, offered from tender little hearts by a three-year-old and a five-year-old, both with blonde hair and enormous blue eyes, from which fall the biggest tears: "Nana, will you die? Nana, my mama died. Don't cry, Nana. Mommy is in heaven; she's watching us and is still smiling! Please, Nana, stay five more minutes, just five more minutes, please!" Oh, the power of words.

On Monday, October 30, 2006, we were reminded of the *power of words*, so I began my journal that day, with these simple but *powerful words* from Psalms 23:1–6 (NIV).

> The Lord is my Shepherd. I shall not be in want. He makes me lie down in green pastures, and he leads me beside the still waters, he restores my soul. Even though I walk through the valley of the shadow of death, I will fear no evil, for you are with me, your rod and your staff, they comfort me. You prepare a table before me in the presence of my enemies. You anoint my head with oil, and my cup overflows. Surely goodness and love will follow me all the days of my life, and I will dwell in the house of the Lord forever.

When I included these words in my journal on that day so many months ago, I had no idea how very close we were to the *valley of the shadow of death*. It became necessary to life flight Laura to Kansas City from Garden City late on the evening of Sunday, October 29, 2006. I had literally just arrived home from western Kansas when I received this news. As a caregiver, you walk a very thin line between wanting to be there to constantly support and encourage and at the same time offer your daughter (or son or spouse or parent) the opportunity to hold onto what little independence they still have. I always felt guilty leaving, and Laura always felt guilty keeping me away from my life back in Kansas City; so against my own instincts, yet with her strong voice of encouragement, I had come home, knowing that they would then be coming to our home in Kansas City, on November 7, as they prepared for their next trip to Duke University.

Laura had enjoyed a reasonably "good" week; the physical challenges of the chemo had not been as intense, but the mental challenges had increased: difficulty reading, spelling, remembering, focusing, processing and communicating information. It was strange the things she could/could not remember. The word *tortilla* was still stuck in her mind, and she continued to confuse it with the word *lock*. We would laugh privately and be saddened that she couldn't remember this simplest of words and then proceed to lock the "tortilla." Even she knew it wasn't right.

During her few "good" days, as always, she wanted to pack as much living into the moments as she possibly could. The weather was beautiful that week, early fall days with the leaves beginning to change colors and just the hint of cold in the air.

We made trips to Wal-Mart and Target. She asked me to stay close to her in the store for fear of losing her bearings. She shopped for cards but was overwhelmed by all of the options. She finally asked me to stand her in front of the baby-girl cards and allow her a moment to focus on the colors and images; it was too challenging to even try to read the words. She wrote words on the calendar and knew they were misspelled, but could not determine what needed to be changed. We met her friend, Paige, and little Carson downtown at Traditions for one of her favorite lunches, the French Dip, and sat on the back porch at Jennifer's and talked and laughed while the kids played in the sand. We shared wonderful, joyful words of encouragement and hope. That week she also walked through the house and asked John to help her hang several photos and prints that she recently had framed and lastly selected colorful new pillows for their sectional in the basement. It seemed she wanted to offer those last decorating touches to their beautiful home. She had so carefully decorated every corner of their little yellow house; she was determined to add the finishing touches before her final days were over.

On Saturday that week, she had offered to host a shower for her friend Wendy Just, who was expecting her first baby. Every detail had to be perfect. We worked all week getting the house in order (Laura directing from the bed, as I fulfilled her requests). John's mom helped with food preparation; her friends assisted with table decorations, and Laura saved her last ounce of energy to put on her "party" clothes. We kept telling her, "Laura, you don't have to do this!" but she wanted to do so. She loved opening her home to others and also thought it would be easier to have friends come to her house than for her to go elsewhere. She looked beautiful that morning. We look at those pictures still and marvel at how amazing she looked in light of what was to come. I drove home Saturday afternoon and late that evening Laura began having more serious side effects from the pressure, new growth, and swelling in her brain. They had invited a few friends over for the evening, just a few close friends and their children in their costumes, celebrating this special fall season. Laura became aware that her speech was becoming difficult, that she was losing her peripheral vision, and that she was losing movement ability on her right side.

Friends went home. John quickly reacted with the meds that he had been instructed to use, and Laura went to sleep. She awoke at four a.m. with a frightening, excruciating headache, and John immediately called the Duke emergency hotline. They were quick to respond and instructed him to take her to the hospital for a CT scan, which he did. The ER doctors in Garden City recommended steroids and morphine. She came home after a few hours and began to regain some of her mobility. However, her thoughts and her ability to communicate words were still coming very slowly. She called us on Sunday morning and could only get a few words out of her mouth, "Mom, it's really bad," and then she began to cry. We knew at that point that we were walking very gently toward the November 9 date for her next assessment by the physicians at Duke. We also knew that their decisive words of her current status would be so critical for the months ahead.

So many had continued to marvel at Laura's strength and our strength, but we knew it was not us. It was the grace of God at work within us. At this point in the journey, we had no strength or courage left of our own. It was God's grace, supplied by the thoughts and prayers of so very many, that was sustaining us. In fact, in the year ahead, I would tell a friend who was going through a similar situation, "Pay attention! This is what 'grace' looks like. This is how you stand, when you have no strength of your own." I went to bed that late October evening, remembering the verse God had given me the night before Laura's second craniotomy nearly two years ago. I had studied this particular passage for my children's ministry lesson that very day. It was the story of the Centurion. He came to Jesus pleading for the life of his servant and said to him with such great faith, "Just say the word and my servant [our daughter, John's wife, Matt and Thomas' sister, our friend] will be healed" (Matthew 8:8, NIV). How we prayed that might be true for our Laura. We never doubted God's ability, just were not sure how he would choose to "heal" her.

Laura remained at home throughout most of the day on the twenty-ninth, but later in the evening the pain once again escalated and reached a level that John was no longer able to manage from home. They returned to the hospital in Garden City with the thought of taking her to Wichita the following morning. However, the Wichita hospital was hesitant to accept her as a patient since she had not previously been treated there. John then began making the arrangements to fly her to Menorah Hospital in Overland Park, Kansas, a hospital that she was familiar with and one that would be able to coordinate well with Duke University.

I had so agonized over not being in Garden City on Saturday evening when the pain had become so much worse, but God knew all along where I needed to be—in Kansas City, where she would remain for the next eight days. Once again we saw evidence of God's amazing provision and foreknowledge. Joe and I drove to Menorah very, very early Monday morning and met our little girl shortly after midnight. She offered a small but simple wave of the hand as we met the ambulance, too exhausted and in too much pain to offer any *words* at all. I sent a brief e-mail late that night to a few close friends, encouraging them not to make a trip to the hospital that evening. I closed with these words, "You do not need to come tonight. We will call if it is that serious." Little did we know how serious it would be. We continued to hold onto hope.

That hope was shattered the following morning when John and I met with the attending neurologist at Menorah. He had reviewed the CT scan and invited us into the family consultation room for his analysis. He was very blunt, offering no gentleness. He simply wanted to communicate that, "This is the end of the road. This is all 'she wrote.' You have done all you can do. Accept what happens next." We received these most *difficult words* that morning when the same physician explained the bleakness of Laura's condition and quietly asked John, "What would you like to do? What are your plans?" We heard more *frightening words* much later in the day when the same doctor informed us in a very abrupt manner that she probably only had days to live. I had always admired John's ability to think rationally and his level-headedness during moments of great crisis, and he demonstrated those attributes again on this most difficult day. Without hesitation he told the neurologist that we would wait for Laura's own physician's assessment before proceeding in any direction.

A few hours later, Dr. Blatt, Laura's original neurosurgeon (the one who began this long journey with us six years ago) stopped by to offer *quiet words* of *compassion* and the smallest glimmer of hope and the appropriate medication to finally bring Laura relief from the pressure and swelling on her brain.

And throughout the day we were carried by the *words of encouragement* and *hope and love and prayer* that family and friends far and near had offered. Even if we had not spoken with them personally, we knew of their love and prayers for us.

Joe and I left the hospital very late Monday evening. Laura was at last resting comfortably and sleeping as she had not slept for days, perhaps weeks. She was heavily medicated in order to ease the horrific pain that she had experienced throughout that long day. John, Matt and Thomas, John's cousin (Dr. Nathan Strandmark from Wichita), and our dear friend, Donny Cosse (whose beautiful young wife died of cancer the very same year Laura was diagnosed) were all camped out for the night vigil. Joe and I decided to go home and rest for a few hours and then return. Donny drove the very important disc with Laura's MRI images to KCI airport that night so that they might be flown overnight via FedEx to arrive at Duke by eight a.m. I was amazed at Donny's determination and willingness to help with this small but important detail, and also amazed at the ability of the aircraft to have these images safely delivered across the country in the early morning hours. We would wait for their *words of recommendation* in the morning. There was even a story in that special FedEx delivery, since it was the father of a friend of Laura's who would pilot the plane that evening, delivering those images to Duke University. Kirby Kraft didn't realize it until the receptionist at the airport later told him the story of the young woman battling brain cancer. Kirby knew immediately that it had to be his Laura and that he had just made that "special delivery" to Duke University. Once again, God's orchestration.

As we went to bed that evening, we knew the next day, John's parents would be driving little Colin and Cooper to Kansas City for moments with their mommy. We prayed for those *tiny words* of explanation that would need to be spoken and then asked that all would lift their *words of prayer* to him.

We watched that day of words come to a close and remembered; "Now you shall speak to him and put the words in his mouth. And I will be with your mouth and with his mouth, and I will teach you what you shall do" (Exodus 4:14–16, NKJV). We waited now for God to show us how to walk through the days ahead with the same beauty and grace that Laura had displayed. We prayed that he would be our mouths and that he would teach us what we should now do. We prayed that *our words* might continue to reflect and showcase his glory. Even though the journey was not ending as we had prayed that it would, God was still God. He was still very much in control; his word would still stand true.

Personal Reflections

Have you considered the power of your very own words? What words have you spoken today that you wish you could retrieve? What words did you fail to say that you wish you had?

_____

_____

_____

How long has it been since you have considered the power of God's Word, especially the power of his spoken Word? Purpose to read and to speak his Word today.

_____

_____

_____

There's nothing in the world that I want more, than to be with you.

—"CC" Bloom (Bette Midler, *Beaches*)

Laura's Cloud
of Witnesses

"Therefore, since we are surrounded by such a great cloud of witnesses, let us throw off everything that hinders and the sin that so easily entangles, and let us run with perseverance the race marked out for us. Let us fix our eyes on Jesus, the author and perfecter of our faith, who for the joy set before him endured the cross, scorning its shame, and sat down at the right hand of the throne of God. Consider him who endured such opposition from sinful men, so that you will not grow weary and lose heart" (Hebrews 12:1–3, NIV).

As a little two-year-old, Laura was so very shy. She was always "young" for her age in school with an early August birthday so that compounded her sensitivity to new things and new people. One of the teachers in her three-year-old Sunday School class, so hurt my feelings as a young mother when she told me that she doubted Laura would ever outgrow her shyness. I wish I could share with that woman now what an incredible young woman of beauty and grace Laura became and how kind she was to the people in her life. She did outgrow her shyness and became such an encourager to others.

Colin has inherited his mother's shyness. Cooper is so personable, has not met a stranger, will speak to almost anyone, and always enjoys having a friend around. Colin, on the other hand, is fearlessly brave about physical feats of strength or endurance but does not like to be the center of attention. He boycotted his first attempt at being a ring bearer and later, at Laura's brother's wedding, made it down the aisle only because he walked with his head down, and then walked out of the church backwards so he did not have to look people directly in the eye. If he is his father's son, who he certainly appears to be, Colin will outgrow his shyness and become comfortable with the "cloud of witnesses" that God draws around him.

I know and believe that God purposed for Laura to come to Kansas City in late October of 2006, for some of her last days of medical attention so she might be surrounded by a whole new "cloud of witnesses," people who needed to see the journey of faith that she had been walking. Her friends and family in Garden City had become very aware in the most recent weeks of how critically ill she was. For them, the change had been slow and gradual. For her Kansas City friends, who only saw Laura on her really "good days," the change they saw at the hospital was drastic. They found it difficult to believe that this friend who always took time to spend with them when she was in town and who always looked so beautiful and so "together" could be lying in a hospital bed with a very uncertain future. And yet she had such profound faith in her future.

John and I were at the Menorah Medical Center all day, every day, of that long week, and we saw a host of new witnesses who received word of Laura's condition and came quickly to her side. I cannot begin to remember or to name them all—friends from high school, friends from college, friends from the neighborhood, friends from church, adult friends, family friends, acquaintances that had been receiving my e-mails, pastors, teachers, and so many more.

I called Laura's dear friend, Vicki, and simply said, "Come." Not an easy thing for a young mother of three at the start of a new school year far away on the coast of North Carolina, but she came and stayed all week by Laura's side, whispering words of hope and understanding, offering a manicure and a pedicure, simply sitting by her side and drying her tears, smiling, praying, loving, listening. As I watched this young woman minister to my daughter, I remembered those closing scenes from the movie *Beaches,* the movie they had loved as young girls, and thought of CC sitting beside Hillary in her last moments. Friends drove in from western Kansas and stayed as long as they could ... Paige and Katie and Amanda. Not only Laura's friends, but John's friends, our friends, people who knew our family or their family—they all came. We would be sitting in the waiting room or outside Laura's room and simply have our breath taken away by the sight of someone coming down the hall or getting off the elevator, someone we had not seen for years who simply came to be a part of her cloud of witnesses. John rarely left her side.

Laura had a beautiful corner room with two walls of glass windows that allowed her to view the gardens and walkways that surrounded Menorah Medical Center. Her room was filled with bouquets of flowers. New ones arrived every day and their fragrance and beauty filled the room. I will forever have images in my mind of John, and so many others, who simply sat beside her bed and listened and waited. I remember Laura's brothers, Matt and Thomas, stretched out on the floor with Cooper and Colin, playing games and watching the trails below and planning adventures for the afternoon. A young friend of mine, Jill Ide, called to see if she could visit and bring her new baby girl, Nora. I encouraged her to do so. When they arrived, Laura was awake and having an unusually good moment. I gently placed this four-week-old baby girl, who was so fresh and new from God's hands, into the arms of my daughter. I will never forget the look of absolute sheer joy that came over Laura's face as she held that tiny baby girl. It was almost as if she knew that this little one had only so recently been in God's presence and she knew that she would be seeing him soon too. What a precious gift that moment became for us all.

Laura and John's CEO friend at Menorah was so kind to offer us some additional space on Laura's floor so that we had a place of retreat for the crowd of family and friends who were there each day. I know it also eased the burden on the hospital by giving us a space in which to gather and talk and share. Otherwise, we would have all been spilling out into the hallways. People were constantly dropping by with food and flowers, toys for the little boys, books of encouragement. All were appreciated, but there were moments when I felt compelled to be in a "party mood" greeting people when all I wanted to do was to be by Laura's side. I was not in a party mood. Several dear friends offered to "hostess" for me and kept vigil in the hallways so that I could remain near Laura while still making sure that all our guests were greeted and thanked for coming. Amazingly, Laura was the one who continued to "hostess" from her hospital bed. She had always loved entertaining in her home, and I simply marveled at how she continued to do just that from her hospital bed, even in her weakened condition.

There was a young woman whose face we did not even see who brought four wonderful dinners from the Olive Garden and left them with the nurse to share with our family. I would later learn that it was Corissa Nelson, who had left those with the most amazing note of encouragement. There was our young photographer friend, Janelle Vano, who stayed as many hours as she could, photographing these last days for Laura. She did not want to intrude, but she captured these moments in only the way that she could do; and knelt and prayed when she was not capturing images on film. There was our pastor friend, Dave Cox, who delivered fresh, hot Krispy Kreme donuts before dawn one morning. Those who were Christians and believers drew strength from Laura's courage as she walked this final journey, and those who were not believers marveled at her ability, our ability, to still testify of God's strength and presence in our lives.

There was an incredible nurse on the evening shift, Jacob

Thomas, with whom we had the joy to share more than one evening. He was a young man of great faith and was the first to ask some of the "hard" questions, asking if Laura and John had taken the opportunity to talk frankly and boldly about the days ahead. They had. It was at that moment that Laura said with such surety, "I know where I'm going. I have the easy part. I regret that I leave John with the hard part."

My e-mail on the first of November stated,

> We have prayed that we might continue to be aware of God's presence all around us, and we have. The doctors at Duke affirmed their support today, of the course of treatment that Laura's neurosurgeon had outlined. Basically, they will continue to use new drugs which will act as a diuretic to decrease the fluid in/around her brain, decrease the swelling, decrease the pain and discomfort, and allow her to ease off the high levels of morphine and perhaps begin to be able to focus and process information again. Another CT scan would be scheduled for Thursday and they hope at that time to be able to get a more accurate read of what is actual new growth and what, perhaps, is new swelling. Her doctor said today, "Because your body has responded, even slightly, we have been able to 'buy' you a few more days." Even a few more days are a gift. In perfect trust, we opened our hearts and our minds and our hands for God to do what only he could do.

On the next day, at 5:00 a.m., I wrote to my own family,

I cannot sleep. Just wanted you to know that we sense the presence of your love for us. We have all spent too many hours in hospitals and homes waiting through long moments like these. The hospital has been so gracious to provide a large gathering room for us so that we can spend time together and allow Laura as much quiet and rest as she needs. Then our little boys will arrive and laughter fills the hallways. We are doing well. I sense that today will be more difficult and that is why I cannot sleep. I know how difficult it is for you to be far away, so just keep sending us your thoughts and prayers. We love you. You have each always made Laura laugh and smile, and we love you for that.

And I received this e-mail response from my youngest brother, Richard, in Boston:

Each time I receive an e-mail from you, I feel like my reply should be written during a very quiet moment, by hand, with a special pen, on really good paper, and that responding via e-mail would just not be sufficient. And of course, I never find the moment, or the pen, or the stationery, and another day and then another week go by. Your courage and faith are amazing and inspiring, and we marvel at the way you and your family and friends are supporting Laura and one another in her struggle.

The days that followed unfolded quickly and left us reeling with more challenging news each day. On Thursday, November 2, I wrote in my e-mail:

To quote our little six-year-old friend, Allison: "This has been a very sad day." Laura had her CT scan early this afternoon, and her neurosurgeon was very quick to arrive with his summary plan of the options. They have considered them carefully, and prayerfully, and believe they will choose for her to have surgery, here, next week. It is not a surgery to cure but rather a surgery to "buy" some precious memory-making time together as a family. To travel to Duke again is too risky; to do nothing would allow them only a few more brief days together, and to return home with only steroids offers them only a hope of a few weeks. They will still consider some final recommendations from Duke's review board in the morning but do not anticipate hearing anything that would change their minds. Please pray for wisdom as they make this very difficult decision and pray that God would graciously give them the gift of time. The surgery in itself is risky even under the best of circumstances. Pray also that few, if any, other debilitating side effects will occur as a result of the surgery. We just ask for a few more weeks/months for Laura to love her husband...and her little boys.

We are exhausted today. We "rested" yesterday, and today we awaited the news we had so feared. But God has been gracious to give Laura and John these last wonderful years together and two little boys, who will become their greatest legacy. As we left this evening, Cooper was helping the RN take mommy's blood pressure and temperature, and Colin was clinging to Daddy's neck and begging for a ride on the big hospital escalator. (Entertainment they do not have in Garden City, Kansas!)

Later in the week, I wrote,

Just sending this to a few, because I want to allow John the privacy and time he needs to make this most difficult decision of his life, but we also want you to pray. John heard from Duke very late this afternoon. His first call was from the physicians' assistants who had walked through every step of this long journey with Laura. They simply called to express their admiration for Laura and John and basically to say "good-bye." As he spoke with these who had so tenderly walked this journey with them, the phone suddenly went dead. John never knew if they had lost their connection or if those on the other end of the line had become so overcome with emotion that the conversation had simply stopped. The second call was from the team of physicians at Duke. They discouraged John from attempting the surgery. It was clear from all the images they had reviewed that the tumor had crossed the mid-line of the brain. Surgery would be far too risky, and there would be far too many challenges that would be even more difficult than loss of life. Our hearts are breaking. John will speak with Dr. Blatt again tomorrow. Pray on. The cry of our hearts today has been, "My Father, if it is possible, may this cup be taken from me" (Matthew 26:39, NIV).

Our cloud of witnesses remained so very faithful in their prayers. They continued to give us the strength to stand and to face what lay ahead. On Saturday, the fourth of November, we learned that there would be no trip to Duke, there would be no more series of chemo, and there would be no surgery. John would take Laura home to Garden City to enjoy the beauty of her last days on earth in the comfort and quiet of her own home. Laura understood, and yet she did not understand. As she listened to Dr. Blatt for the last time, she smiled softly and nodded her understanding. It was almost as if she knew her "bags were packed" and she was ready to enter her heavenly home. Moments later, I found myself in the hallway comforting Dr. Blatt's assistant who had become overwrought with emotion herself. She apologized for her tears, and I told her that was not necessary. Their team had so beautifully cared for and so loved our Laura through all these long years there was no need to apologize for the tears.

In those days at Menorah, I had taken the advice of a friend and made time each day for a walk through the beautiful trails and gardens that surrounded the hospital. Those late fall days had added a rich and colorful beauty to the trees in the court-yard. The colors had been absolutely gorgeous all week, but I knew that they paled in comparison to what awaited Laura in the days ahead, in heaven. We could only imagine.

The doctors estimated that it would take three to six weeks for Laura to let go of the things of earth and grasp hold of the things of heaven. "Therefore, we do not lose heart. Though outwardly we are wasting away, yet inwardly we are being renewed day by day. For our light and momentary troubles are achieving for us an eternal glory that far outweighs them all. So we fix our eyes not on what is seen, but on what is unseen. For what is seen is temporary, but what is unseen is eternal" (2 Corinthians 4:16–18, NIV). Laura is another day closer to him.

We were at the hospital early on Monday morning, November 5, to help pack Laura for her final trip home. We had to smile because even in her fragile state she still offered direction to us as she always had. She asked that the first stop after we left the hospital be PF Chang's restaurant on the Plaza in Kansas City for Chinese food. Their trips to Duke had always included a stay at a lovely hotel and then dinner at PF Chang's in Raleigh-Durham. Laura had asked John for the last few days if they would be going out to eat. John decided to make this one last wish come true before she left Kansas City.

It was clear that she was already becoming "absent" from the body. Although she was physically still with us, we sensed that she was also beginning to slip away from us. We thanked the host of people who had gathered around us in Kansas City and knew that we would have another cloud of witnesses ready to greet us in Garden City. Hospice would be called and would be awaiting our arrival too. It was difficult to imagine that only eight days earlier we had been shopping in town, enjoying lunch with friends, and relaxing on the patio while the kids laughed and played. God had given us so many absolutely beautiful fall days to enjoy before she began her journey home. We were thankful for that.

During these last days, we were blessed with his grace and with "the peace of God which transcends all understanding" (Philippians 4:7, NIV). A sweet friend reminded me as I left the hospital that when Laura was first diagnosed with brain cancer I had given her a small plaque, which had been resting beside her bathroom sink all these years. It said very simply, "Laura, trust me. I have everything under control. Love, Jesus." She had faithfully trusted him every day of this journey and now was nearly home. I closed my e-mail with, "Pray on for the impact this one life will have upon all the lives she has touched, for she has left her handprint on so very many hearts. Thank you, God, for her amazing cloud of witnesses, people who will remember and keep her memory alive."

Personal Reflections

Who are the people that God has drawn around you as your personal "cloud of witnesses"?

_____

_____

_____

What testimony are they seeing lived out in you? Are you remembering to "showcase," to reflect, to honor the Author and Creator of your life?

_____

_____

_____

And so we wait for heaven to come to earth.

Final Days
at Home

"Do not let your hearts be troubled. Trust in God; trust also in me. In my Father's house are many rooms; if it were not so, I would have told you. I am going there to prepare a place for you." (John 14:1–3, NIV).

I had done really well most of the week until I sat down one night to read Colin his bedtime stories, and he had chosen *Mommies Are for Counting Stars*.[21] The story reads, "A mommy is nice to sit on; and nice to lean on; a mommy knows how to kiss a boo-boo; a mommy always waits for you to come home; mommies give baths and comb your hair; and if there's some-place for you to go, a mommy will take you there." I lost my emotions there and had to remind myself that Laura had done all those things and that daddies could do all these things too.

The trip home from Kansas City to western Kansas was so very hard. After lunch at PF Chang's, we pushed Laura in her wheelchair to the curb outside the restaurant and safely tucked her into the car. Laura and her little boys rode in the Suburban with John and Grandma Jan (John's mother) and Aunt Jennifer (John's sister). I walked back to my car in the parking garage, said my good-byes to our family, and then left only moments after the Suburban. I kept thinking I would catch up with them or hear from them or be invited to stop for a moment so that we could trade passengers or drivers, but I never saw or heard from them on the highway that long afternoon. I knew they were so very focused on their patient, along with keeping Cooper and Colin entertained in the car, but I thought for sure I would receive a phone call. Our worlds had all changed. We were all adjusting to what would be "our new normal." In earlier days, Laura would have been calling me every hour, updating me on what was happening, and checking on my safety and my anticipated arrival time. All that would now change. I knew that and understood, but it was one more small reminder of how drastically our lives were about to change.

They had sent us home with the hope of six to eight weeks of "last days" with Laura, but we were given the gift of only eight days. She had rested for eight days in Kansas City, and now would have eight final days in Garden City. We met the wonderful hospice team that services the people in the Garden City area. We thought these would be individuals with whom we would establish a long relationship over many weeks, but that was not to be.

On Saturday, November 11, at three thirty in the afternoon, I wrote:

> We are safely home in western Kansas and have enjoyed the beauty of these incredibly gorgeous summer-like fall days. Laura has even been able to sit outside on the porch a few times while she visited with friends and watch the beauty of the sky and the clouds. We have had several visits from hospice already. They have carefully outlined the care that they will provide, and we have a nurse coming by each week. John and Laura's pastor also came one day and spent a long time simply being available to them both. And through each of our days, they have been surrounded by more family and friends who love them so dearly and whose lives have been touched by Laura.
>
> As we left Kansas City on Monday, I quietly began making my "last times" list: the last time she would be at Menorah Medical Center, the last time she would enjoy an afternoon on the Plaza, the last time she would see her friend Vicki, the last time she would spend time at our house, the last time she would drive across the state of Kansas, the last time she would eat at PF Chang's—silly the things your mind thinks about when your heart is burdened with so very much. Laura now feels "drugged." She slips in and out of real awareness. She has some lucid moments and then moments when even she knows she isn't making any sense, but we all try to understand. The medications seem to be doing

a good job helping her manage her pain, and we are thankful for that. We are each simply looking for moments to remember in each new day. She rode with John today to take Cooper to preschool and loves these small moments that remind her when life was "normal." We often find her with tears streaming down her face when she hears a dear friend's voice on the phone or when she watches her brothers, Matt and Thomas, playing with Colin and Cooper on the floor, or when she sees her dad walk in the door.

We have continued to see the hand of God all around us and know that he is still very much in control. He is not surprised by what is happening. Acts 26:16 has been a powerful verse for me this past year, and I know that these words are applicable to all that we have experienced in these past months. "Now, get up and stand on your feet! I have appeared to you to appoint you as a servant and as a witness of what you have seen of me and what I will show you" (NIV). When we have had no strength, he has supplied us with what we have needed for the day. We have seen so much. We have experienced so much. And we will have much to testify about in the days and months ahead. Most of all, we will speak of his faithfulness and his love and his provision. Remember, this is not Laura's story, or ours; it is God's story about his amazing love. This journey has simply been the part that has included us. We are praying that we will be found faithful.

In the days that followed, a sweet and thoughtful friend from their church brought Cooper and Colin two small stuffed animals—an elephant and a lion, an elephant because they never forget and a lion because of their bravery. What a precious thought for two little boys to cling to during the long days ahead; it was a precious thought for the grownups too. Be strong and brave. Do not forget. Over the weekend many friends and family traveled from far and near to see Laura for one last time. My sister, Sue, took precious time out of her busy life to drive Laura's elderly Aunt Joan and Uncle Billy to Garden City for final words of good-bye. Several of Laura's college friends arrived for a tour of the farm and for lunch in Garden City. They so wanted to capture in a few brief days what Laura had been experiencing for years. Laura's dad and her brothers came back for the weekend, thinking they would be back again before she left this earth. Her prayer group gathered that Sunday evening and offered prayers of hope for Laura, and even Laura prayed for John, for Colin and Cooper, and for all that lay ahead.

One of my last memories of Laura will always be a moment we shared on the sofa in her living room on one of her last days at home. John had given Laura her medications for the morning, Cooper was at school, and Colin was playing with a friend. Laura was awake, but oh so quietly resting on the sofa. I sat on the floor beside her and gently filed her beautiful, long fingernails; remarkably, this was one of the last things I remember doing for my mother as well. I reminded Laura that many people were still praying for a "miracle" for her, and she reminded me that she believed she would know when it would be time to "let go." I knew in that moment how important it was for me to affirm this knowledge for her, and I did. I assured her that God would whisper to her heart when the time would be right to let go of the things of this earth and to embrace the things of heaven. We did not doubt that God still had the power to turn the forces of this disease completely around and to heal her body, but we also knew that we did not know how he might choose to showcase his glory. In Laura's case, we were being drawn to the conclusion that his glory and majesty would be magnified in Laura's untimely and early death. We thanked the individuals who continued to pray for miracles, but we also embraced the few who were brave enough to know that these were Laura's very last days. And so I swallowed deeply and embraced my daughter and agreed with her that God would direct her in when it was time to go. We would not cling or beg or deny; she had always only been loaned to us for a little while.

It is Tuesday morning. We are watching as Laura is gracious in the way that she leaves us, just as she has been gracious in the way that she has lived each day of her life. We enjoyed a wonderful weekend with family and friends. Then, yesterday morning, she awoke with an extreme headache and was unable to even get out of bed. John began increasing the pain medication dosages as he had been instructed to do, and we waited. We knew the drugs themselves would put her into a deep sleep and a period of rest, but long after the effectiveness of the drugs had passed she continued to sleep.

John called the hospice nurse to stop by early this morning, and even she was surprised at the dramatic change since last Friday. We really cannot conceive of eight weeks of waiting but also are not ready to let her go. Laura is unresponsive. Her pupils are fixed and dilated; her breathing is very slow. She is still wearing her pain patch and does not appear to be in any physical pain, sleeping peacefully in her bed. She has not received any steroids for some time now, and that has been the only thing that had offered any containment of the swelling. Her doctors in Kansas City had told us that when it reached this point she would probably be gone from us within one to three days. And so we wait on heaven to come to earth.

Our hearts are breaking, but we are confident that she is already beginning her journey to a far, far better place. She doesn't leave us; she is simply going before us. As I stood over her this morning, stroking the little bit of hair that still remains around her beautiful face, I simply kept thinking, *She has fought the good fight, she is finishing the race, she has kept the faith, and now there is in store for her the crown of righteousness, which the Lord, the righteous judge, will award to her on that day, and not only to her, but also to all who have longed for his appearing* (2 Timothy 4:7–8, NIV).

In the last months, when Laura had faced the enormity of her journey, I had given her a copy of Don Piper's book *Ninety Minutes in Heaven*,[22] the true story of a man who was declared clinically dead after a horrific car accident but who lived to tell of the ninety amazing, incredible minutes he experienced in heaven. I encouraged Laura to specifically read the first three chapters, which speak of the miracle of heaven, the music of heaven, and the people of heaven. I so wanted her to have that image in her mind as she walked her final days on earth. She knew that her presence in heaven would be instantaneous and that she would be surrounded by the most incredible music of praise and worship and that she would see the faces of people who had gone before her into God's presence. All of that awaited her in the days ahead and brought her great comfort.

During those last days, we took turns caring for the boys and sitting beside Laura as she slept quietly in her bed. I found moments throughout the day to rest beside her and gently stroke the little bits of hair that remained on her head and whisper to her the words that I wanted her to hear. I remembered being told that your hearing is one of the last senses to function, so I longed for her to hear in her last moments words of love and hope and encouragement and faith. I believe that she did.

Laura was visited by many friends on those last days; they would come for moments, offer prayers, and then slip away to allow another friend or loved one to draw near. At about eight that evening, I began the bedtime routine of pajamas and bedtime stories and a bottle for Colin and then bed. After the boys were asleep, we gathered in Laura's room to listen as she took her final breaths. Outside our windows, a violent wind storm began to make its presence known. In those last moments with Laura, the wind blew so violently we could hear the sound of tumbleweeds as they were picked up by the wind and then thrown against the outside of the house with a terrific force. It was the strangest sound I had ever heard and one I will never forget as heaven came to earth that night. We awakened to piles of tumbleweeds on our front porch, and that morning I wrote:

Our sweet, precious Laura went home to heaven

last night, November 14, at about 9:15 p.m. She quietly, and so thoughtfully, waited until her two little boys were safely tucked into bed before taking those last long breaths. She was surrounded by people who loved her dearly. We think of the host that welcomed her home and are so very thankful that she knew with certainty and assurance where she would spend eternity.

God granted us an absolutely beautiful blue sky day for Laura's memorial service in western Kansas, and I wrote that evening:

We are just home from the celebration of Laura's life, and just wanted you to each know how profoundly we have sensed your presence with each of us today as we walked this difficult but oh so memorable day. God was very much with us. He was honored and glorified as we offered our tributes to Laura. We had shared with their pastor on Wednesday that this simply had to be a unique, never-to-be-forgotten celebration of her life and the impact she has had on the lives of so many others because of her faith. It was. The music, the words that God enabled us to speak, the thoughts that were shared, the amazing flowers, and the "great cloud of witnesses" all contributed to the beauty of this day.

What is the measure of one life well lived? Twelve hundred in attendance at the services for this young, thirty-year-old woman? One hundred seven floral arrangements? Over four hundred sympathy cards? One thousand extra cell-phone minutes on her mother's cell phone? One grieving husband and two little boys pointing at the images of their mommy on the screen and crying out, "My mama" as they patted their little hearts. One life yielded to him, the God of the universe. Laura was extraordinary in her ordinariness. She was not well traveled, she did not pursue fame or fortune, she did not long for personal acknowledgement or recognition, she simply recognized each day for the treasure that it was and longed to bring glory to God with each breath that she took. She did that by loving him, by loving her family, by loving her husband and her precious little boys, by caring for the people in her life, by laughing, by dancing, by smiling and winking and remembering how precious each day was. She did each of these so well.

John and Colin and Cooper left our house after the second memorial service in Kansas City on a Tuesday, and packing them all in the car was a sad, sad thing. I told the boys that I would be coming out in a few days, and Cooper looked at me with tears streaming down his face and simply said, "Nana, this is not a good idea! *Not* a good idea." Colin just kept patting the seat next to him as if to say, "Sit here, Nana," and then began to cry when he saw Cooper's tears.

I had already told John a truth I knew so well. I had told him that he would want the world to come to a *stop*. I had first experienced this emotion in 1994 when my father had died of a sudden and massive heart attack. I remembered driving down the street of one of the main thoroughfares near my home, thinking, *Why are these people in their cars driving around? Don't they know someone great has died? How could they possibly still be engaged in life?* I then realized I was driving as well. You wish the world would stop so that your heart could have the time it needs to grieve; but the realities of life continue to pull you forward, and that in time allows your heart to begin to heal. And that is exactly what God had planned. The realities of life for John would be simple ones: Cooper would need his juice cup filled and would need something for show'n tell, Colin would need a diaper change and help finding his missing pacifier, they would both want to go outside to ride their bikes and trikes, the cattle would need to be fed, and work would resume for us all. Slowly we would all be pulled back into *life*, and that is what Laura would have wanted and what God had designed.

Personal Reflections

What things are troubling your heart today? Do you trust in him? Do you have the assurance that he does go to prepare a place for you and that he will come again and take you to be with him? If not, accept his invitation today.

_____

_____

_____

_____

_____

All roads begin and end with this fact:

she is gone...

Remembering the Early Days of Grief

"Do not let your hearts be troubled ... And if I go and prepare a place for you, I will come back and take you to be with me that you also may be where I am" (John 14:1–3, NIV).

A friend recently asked me, "When did the joy return? How long did it take for the overwhelming pain of this great loss to leave you and for the joy to return?"

My reply was simple, "It never left. The joy was always there ... every day." Even in the early moments of such great pain, we were still able to find something to smile about, something to remember, something to laugh out loud about, something to cherish. Laura loved to play "peek-a-boo" with the boys and especially with "baby" Colin, even in those last days. She would open the door from the bedroom, and if the boys were already awake, she would place her hands over her eyes and walk out of her bedroom with those words on her lips ... "peek-a-boo!" And a big smile would fill Colin's face. Or she might cuddle up on the sofa and hide her face behind one of their big pillows and surprise the boys when they awoke from their naps with a loud "peek-a-boo!" Our "joy" was like that as well, surprising us at moments when we were not expecting to laugh, making us smile, and peeking its head through that heavy curtain of grief.

In those early days of December 2006, we got up each day and tried to imagine what the rest of our lives would look like. In the weeks ahead, I would learn that all roads begin and end with this fact: she is gone. And I would later learn that no matter how much new *joy* I would pour into my life—and there would be much joy—nothing could "fill" the void that I would feel. No amount of joy could replace the fact that she was gone. And then there would be so many days when I would question, is she really gone? How can it be? I still hear her voice in my head and see her face before me.

In the months that followed, we took Cooper and Colin to visit their mommy's grave, and Cooper was sure that they had spelled his name incorrectly, since the engravers had chiseled "COOPER" instead of "Cooper." Colin would simply pat his little heart and say, "My mama." One day when we took flowers to Laura's grave, Cooper needed to make an emergency bathroom stop. I drove hurriedly through the cemetery, but realized quickly that there were no public restrooms. I knew Cooper could not wait, so I circled back around, ran with him to a beautiful, large tree near mommy's grave, and gave him a moment to "water" the greenery. Laura would have laughed. I'm sure she did.

Moments with my little boys made me laugh or cry each day. I will always remember the first Christmas without Laura. I was helping John and the boys decorate the tree with the ornaments that Laura had collected throughout the years. While tears collected in my own eyes, Cooper raced around the tree with his Santa hat on his head and his Santa bag hanging over his shoulder. He saw the tears in my eyes and said in his little cautionary voice, "Don't cry Nana! Mommy is in heaven watching us, and she's smiling 'cause we're putting up the tree!" A few weeks later, I was reading bedtime stories to the boys, and Colin and I were resting in the lower section of Cooper's trundle bed. When the stories were all done and prayers had been said, Colin began frantically trying to communicate a thought to me in his little two-year-old voice, "Nana, you, us, you, live…" I struggled to understand what he was trying to say to me and finally asked, "Colin, do you want me to live where you live?" His tears and his hugs and the end of his sobbing told me all I needed to know. *Yes, Nana should live where Colin lives.*

Months passed. I kept thinking that I would write just one more e-mail, and then the words would continue to pour out of my heart. God continued to stir my heart to send just "one more." Perhaps because he knew it allowed me the opportunity to simply acknowledge and honor the strength of God that continued to flow through me. I headed back to western Kansas on a Sunday afternoon in early March. This would have been my third trip since Laura's passing. I looked forward to each trip with both joy and sadness, knowing much joy awaited me there but also knowing that things would never be the same. It was as difficult for me to travel west as it was for John to come to our house in Kansas City. Each location held different, poignant memories for each of us.

In those early days of grief, I felt that my heart was most protected when I was at home surrounded by my own secure walls and by the people who encouraged and supported me and by the routines of my daily life. When I traveled west or south to visit family, I somehow felt "unprotected." My heart was more vulnerable, and I sensed myself drawing within myself. Those around me didn't know what to do or say, so they said nothing. Laura's passing frequently was the "elephant" in the room that no one wanted to acknowledge, and that hurt worst of all. It was just one more reminder that everyone else's life was moving forward and that ours was standing still.

I began to learn to fill my days but not my heart ... not yet. I had been spending some time on two part-time "jobs," one with a small company owned by dear friends who were allowing me the opportunity for creative and inspirational input into their company's future, and I also was fulfilling a very small ministry position at our church. As I drove to work one morning, I paused in the parking lot and thought how gracious God had been to allow me these opportunities—reasons to get out of bed and add meaning and purpose to my life. I would not have been able emotionally to even think about pursuing a new position or putting together a résumé, but both positions were laid before me so easily, and both had been so gracious in their flexibility and understanding. I was so thankful. I was so grateful. They were essential to my emotional survival. Plus both positions also afforded me the opportunity to spend a week every five weeks or so with my two grandsons, trips that were so very necessary for my sanity.

I learned to balance new days and so many old memories. We would sit and sift through pictures of all of us, even just from the last summer and would marvel at how amazing Laura had looked. And then in those later pictures, we watched her "decline" in pictures from September and October. The blank look in her eyes began to warn us that she was becoming more and more absent from the body and present with the Lord. New days, old memories. John said he felt as if he were "drowning." Life had lost its "flavor"— his words, not mine. He said it was as unpleasant as eating food without any seasoning—no salt, no pepper—nothing to add the "spice" to life. He also said that he had lost his "drive," his purpose; he had lost his motivation for all that he did. Laura was all that and so much more. We began to pray that John would find someone to love again. We knew that had also been Laura's prayer. John doubted that would ever happen, especially in the small community in which he lived, but I reminded him that he was underestimating the power of what God could do. John was much too young not to find love again, and our little boys needed a mother to smother them with kisses and hugs, to whisper words of love to them, to listen to their bedtime prayers, and to cuddle with them in the early morning hours. There were too many lonely hearts in that household. We did not doubt that God would hear our prayers for a new love.

I also learned how to answer the question, "How many children do you have?" I met new people in my places of employment and new people at church, and of course the first question we always ask one another is, "How many children do you have?" A very simple question unless you have recently lost a child. I wondered what the simple answer to that question might be. And I was also so thankful for my amazing sons and prayed daily for love and laughter, joy, and fulfillment for both of them. I also became increasingly aware of the young people (particularly young women) and the "young" friendships in my life, precious lives that I had the opportunity to still mentor and to encourage.

I was not ready for spring. Everyone else was, but I was not. It was March; spring was coming. But spring would be a sign of new life, new beginnings. We were still in "winter." Spring was a sign that everyone was moving forward, while I was standing still. I did not want to see the leaves come back onto the trees, for the birds to begin their morning songs, or for the spring flowers to begin blooming; all were reminders of a rebirth. Laura was gone; this was a spring she would not enjoy on this side of heaven. That became true for every season. Laura loved summer best of all: shorts and sandals, bike rides and sundresses, and walks along the beach and afternoons at the pool. *How could I handle a summer without Laura?*

There were the little things that only a "Nana" would notice; a small understanding that the little boys no longer had their mommy's voice whispering in their heads about the people in Kansas City who loved them so very much. Just the smallest differences that again magnify our loss. Laura and I had talked daily, many times twice a day, and she was careful to always let the little boys speak to me on the phone or to leave me messages. She was no longer able to do that, and John did not have the time to even think about doing it. I understood, but still it was hard not to hear those little voices in my ear or on my answering machine. Even today, at four o'clock, I still will think about calling her because if we had not talked during the day that would be the time we would check in with one another.

In my Valentine's Day card, Joe had written that he missed the innocence we had before this profound loss had touched our lives. So well said; the innocence we had before Laura left us. *Was she really gone?* It was still so very hard to fathom.

I felt a kinship with the early pioneers; always packing my suitcase with casseroles for the week ahead; food for the journey, treats for Colin and Cooper; clothes for the playground, the zoo, and the new trampoline; playdough and bubbles and paints to fill our afternoons; notes of encouragement from friends to share with John; thoughts in my head and heart to share with Laura's dear friends; and music for the drive to inspire my soul and soften the soil of my heart. I was always glad that my "wagon" provided better comfort and shelter than those of the early pioneers, who had first made those long trips back and forth across our wide state. I thought of those pioneers so often as I drove up and over the rolling plains of Kansas. I had specific prayer warriors that faithfully prayed for me as I drove (thank you, Lois) that angels would surround my car and keep me safe and awake. They did. I never traveled "alone."

I wrote a synopsis about my grief. I did not share the

words with anyone. Simply putting the words on paper eased my pain. I called it Grief 101.

Grief 101
Walking through the "Early Days"

1. I want the world to stop, but it does not.

2. People do not know what to say to me, so many say nothing. Some even avoid me.

3. Friends ask me how I am doing, and they want me to say, "I am fine." I need them to ask and then ask that question again, so that I can tell them how I really feel.

4. My loss has broken my heart. But it has also broken the heart of God. I lost my only daughter. He lost his one and only Son. I cry over my great physical loss. He cries over the great spiritual loss of those who are truly "lost."

5. I have totally unplugged from my life. My own life is on hold, and it is so difficult for me to "plug back in."

6. I just want to recapture the beauty of an ordinary, normal day.

7. As time passes, I wonder if everyone else has forgotten our loss.

8. Remarkably, comforting someone else brings comfort to my own heart.

9. Some friends say, "Call me if I can help!" but they never come, they never invite me out, they never allow me to talk. My grief has immobilized me. I need them to take the initiative.

10. People say I am so brave, so strong. I am not. God is.

11. I need to embrace the pain. Each tear I cry adds to the healing of my heart. I still cry tears today. I think that will always be the case.

12. I don't normally cry easily; still, I have cried gallons of tears. The tears often come in the early-morning hours or the late-night hours or when I am in my car…"sanctuary" moments, just me and God.

13. As time passes, I will realize that I am having more "good" days than "bad" days. Will that happen soon?

14. There is so much pressure to put on a happy face and to be "normal" again. I don't feel normal.

15. I cannot seem to get my head and my heart on the same page. It is the first thought in the morning and the last thought at night…*she is gone.* I will see her again, but she is gone.

You will want the world to stop, but it does not. In time, the realities of life will begin to pull you forward, and that, with God's great grace, will allow your heart to begin to heal.

How very thankful I was that God had given John two boys, not girls who would have needed bows to be tied and long hair to be combed and dresses to be ironed and dolls to be dressed; but boys, who could survive in "farm" clothes, although he always dressed them well. He would have managed girls beautifully, but how wise of God to give him boys.

Just about this time, the Kleenex company launched a new ad campaign, which involved placing a huge, comfortable sofa in the middle of a downtown area and then simply supplying a box of tissues for passersby as they answered questions and talked about their lives. I will never forget the image of one young woman crying her eyes out as she sat at the end of the sofa and then commenting, "My tears do not diminish my strength." I loved that. Typically, before Laura's passing, I was not one who cried easily, but now I had cried gallons of tears.

I loved saying, "My tears do not diminish, do not negate, do not decrease, do not wipe away the strength of God which flows through me!" Every tear that I cried added and aided in my healing, so I encouraged the tears to flow.

A friend just recently asked me, "When did the tears stop?"

And I quietly replied, "I still cry tears today, every day. Something...a word, a note, a song, a picture, a memory...something will move me to tears, and I cry."

My mother had lost a child. My oldest brother, Michael, died only six weeks after our father had died, that had been nearly thirteen years ago. Michael was forty-eight at the time and died of a massive heart attack. He left behind a grieving wife and two young sons, ages five and seven. I watched my mother and my sister-in-law grieve and thought I understood, but I did not. This is an understanding that you can only fathom after taking those same steps yourself. My brother, Robert, wrote a poem for me just after we had lost Laura. My mother would have loved it:

> It wasn't supposed to be this way, my mother told me so.
> You see, like me she lost a child before her time to go. I
> know she's in a better place, away from all the pain. I'll
> keep her safe within my heart, sweet memories remain.

I can vividly remember my mother, standing beside the phone in her kitchen, sharing with me how very difficult this loss had been. She had buried her husband (of over fifty years) our father, only weeks before. But the loss of her firstborn had cut so much more deeply into her heart. As we mature and walk through life, we know that losing our spouse will one day occur, but you never anticipate that your child will be struck down in the most incredible and significant time of her life.

"I miss Laura." I wrote those words after she had been in heaven for 351 days. I miss her still today. I cannot say that loudly enough. I miss her. John misses her. Her little boys miss her. We all miss her. Cooper would later say, "I miss my mommy even when I don't cry." We miss her presence, we miss her hands, we miss her kisses, we miss her heart, we miss her smiles, we miss her winks, we miss her beauty, and we miss her voice. In those first early days of grief, John searched the house frantically for a stuffed teddy bear that he and Laura and Cooper had made for Colin on his first birthday at the Build-A-Bear Workshop. John wanted that bear because they had also carefully recorded a voice message to Colin and then tucked that voice chip inside the little bear's hand. "Happy Birthday, Colin! Love you!" Those words, spoken in Laura's voice, were so powerful. It is also why, for the next two years you could still hear Laura's voice on the telephone answering machine saying, "You've reached the Kleysteubers! Leave a message, and we'll call you back!"

All too soon the months had quickly passed, and it was time to celebrate Laura's life and to remember her passing on the one-year anniversary of her death. Laura's dad and I and her brothers were all in Kansas City that day, so we did not have her house to visit or her cemetery plot to lay flowers upon, so we created a "memory walk" to remember this special day and this precious life.

I asked each of our family members to clear that day on their calendar: no meetings, no phone calls, no commitments, and so we did. I then purchased twelve beautiful white, long-stem roses. We agreed to all meet at one of our very favorite breakfast places, First Watch; a place that Laura had often enjoyed eating at with our family. Our dear pastor friend, Donnie Simpson, met us too, in addition to Thomas' lovely Karen (who on the following day would become his fiancé). We enjoyed a wonderful breakfast together and began by telling stories of Laura's life. Before we left, I handed one of those lovely long-stemmed roses to our young waitress and told her briefly why we were there and what we would be doing that day. I encouraged her to enjoy the beauty of this day, this moment, this gift from God.

We next went to Emmanuel Baptist Church, the church where Laura and John had been married and the place where she had enjoyed so many activities as a little girl and as a teenager. We stopped in the office to let them know what we were doing, and then took our time walking the hallways and looking in classrooms, remembering. We began in the sanctuary, with the placement of a rose on the altar and with some special words that we shared with one another and then a prayer of thanksgiving for her life. We walked through every corner of that building, which was filled with so many "Laura" memories.

Our third stop was an important one—Menorah Medical Center. We did not have a graveside to visit in Kansas City, but we had wanted some kind of a "memorial" location, so we had placed a beautiful "stepping stone" in the gardens at Menorah. The stone simply said, "Laura Kleysteuber, August 5, 1976–November 14, 2006, We remember her endurance inspired by hope. 1 Thess. 1:3" It rests under a beautiful tree beside a quiet stream near a small bridge just past the butterfly garden. We laid several roses there and paused to remember her room and all the memories of the eight days she had spent at this facility.

We drove by our first home in Lenexa, the house in which Laura had grown up, and laid flowers at the curbside. We stopped at a location near Vicki's old house and remembered all the moments she had spent there with her precious friend. We visited her old elementary school and had a wonderful visit with the principal, again explaining our purpose and were welcomed with open arms. Laura's brothers had so much fun exploring the old classrooms and hallways and cafeteria and gymnasium from their early childhood days too. We also stopped by their high school at the end of the school day and walked more hallways reminiscing about all the dances and basketball games and classes and parties that had been such an important part of Laura's life.

At the end of the day, our last stop was for dinner at PF Chang's on the Country Club Plaza. My last rose was looking a little "sad" at that point, but we immediately told the hostess what we were doing and handed her the rose. We smiled as she found a vase for it and fresh water and placed it prominently on her hostess stand. We then watched that rose throughout the evening as new life came back into that fragile flower.

Oh how we missed her and how we miss her still, but we

all also know with assurance that she is in a far, far better place and that one day we will see her again. We truly believe that she is not gone, she is simply gone from us and she has gone before us. In a very real sense, I believe that she has stepped through that thin veil that separates heaven and earth. She is very much "alive." But we cannot see her face or hear her voice or watch her dance. I know with full assurance that she is in heaven and that I will see her someday. I personally believe that she is doing wonderful things that perfectly align with the ways in which she was so gifted here on earth. I know that she is busy and active and winking and smiling, fulfilling her role in heaven, just as she did on earth.

Years earlier a friend had shared the following words with me and encouraged me to fill in the blank with my own name, knowing what encouragement these words would bring to me: "Sandy, you take care of the things that are precious to me, and I will take care of the things that are precious to you. Love, God." He had. He faithfully had. I knew that I would still long for the world to stop, but I also knew that my life still had meaning and purpose in and of itself. The realities of life would continue to pull me forward and that in time and with God's grace would allow my heart to begin to heal.

Just in these very last days, I was dusting my shelves and looked again at a picture of Laura that I have in which she is wearing her pink bandana with very little hair and holding one of her boys on her lap. The picture was taken during one of her very last days on earth. The words on the frame simply say, "To change the world a mother needs only to put hope in the heart of a child." I am thankful for the hope that Laura's dad and I had been able to place in Laura's heart; and I knew that even in the few short years that she had lived Laura had placed hope in the hearts of her boys. Perhaps we truly might be able to change the world. Hope draws us forward not because it promises a better tomorrow, but because it causes us to watch for God's presence and his power even when life does not proceed as we have planned. That is hope. That is the truth that Laura held onto, and that is why we will always remember. *Behind the beauty and the grace, behind the winks and the smiles, there was always hope.*

Personal Reflections

For what people or circumstances or things have you most recently grieved? A lost child, a lost love, a lost job opportunity, a lost dream? We grieve over each of these. What has been your most recent loss?

_____

_____

_____

In whose heart are you planting hope? And where does your hope lie?

_____

_____

_____

End Notes

1. "Grace." (Online) http;//www.webster-dictionary.net, August 2008.
2. Sponberg, Nicol. "Resurrection" Audio CD, Curb Records Label, Track #3 "Resurrection," Release Date 2007.
3. Nordeman, Nichole. "Woven and Spun" Audio CD, Sparrow Label, Track # 4 "Legacy," Release Date 2002.
4. Giglio, Louie. *i am not but i know I AM, welcome to the story of God.* Sisters, Oregon: Multnomah Publishers,2005, p.13.
5. "Remember." (Online) http;//www.webster-dictionary.net, August 2008.
6. Karon, Jan. Patches of Godlight. New York, New York. Penguin Publishing Group, 2001, p. 8.
7. Swindoll, Charles. *Perfect Trust.* Nashville, Tennessee: J. Countryman Publishing, 2000, p. 16.
8. Ibid

9. Chapman, Steven Curtis. "More to this Life" Audio CD, Capital Label, Track #5 "I will be here," Release Date 1989.

10. Giglio, Louie. *i am not but i know I AM, welcome to the story of God*. Sisters, Oregon: Multnomah Publishers,2005, p.13.

11. *Contagious Joy*. Nashville, Tennessee: Word Publishing Group. "Unspeakable Joy" by Mary Graham, pp. 86–87.

12. Karon, Jan. Patches of Godlight. New York, New York. Penguin Publishing Group, 2001, p. 8.

13. Adoniram Judson, American Baptist missionary to Burma for forty years. 1788–1850. Translated Bible to Burmese.

14. Buchanan, Sue and Hodges, Lynn. *Dear God, It's Me*. Grand Rapids, Michigan: Zonderkidz, 2005, pp. 1–4.

15. Moore, Beth. Jesus, *Ninety Days with the One and Only*. Nashville, Tennessee: B & H Publishing Group, 2007, p. 83.

16. Nordeman, Nichole. *Woven and Spun* Audio CD, Sparrow Label, Track # 5 "I AM," Release Date 2002.

17. Watchman Nee, 1903–1972, Missionary to China.

18. Norman, Bebo. *Try* Audio CD, Essential label, Track #11 "Borrow Mine," Release Date 2004.

19. Lucado, Max, spoken at "Contagious Joy" Women of Faith Conference, Denver,Colorado, September 2006.

20. Rice, Chris. *Run the Earth; Watch the Sky* Audio CD, Rocketown Label, Track #4 "Untitled Hymn (Come to Jesus), Release Date 2003.

21. Jaber, Cynthia and Harriet Ziefert. *Mommies Are for Counting Stars*. Puffin Books, 1999, pp. 1–5.

22. Piper, Don with Cecile Murphy. *Ninety Minutes in Heaven*. Grand Rapids, Michigan: Fleming H. Revell, a division of Baker Publishing Group, 2004.

Photos

Laura, in the fall of 1996, the year she fell in love with John.

Laura and John's wedding day, August 7ᵗʰ, 1998

Laura's beautiful smile

John, Laura, Cooper, and Colin on the farm 2005

Laura and her boys enjoy a moment of fun, after one of her Dr. appointments in KCity.

Fall 2004... the night before her 2nd craniotomy;
"positioning points" for the surgery, in place.

Laura's famous "wink and a smile"

Down by the creek at Nana's house, with Cooper

*Laura leading the Fiesta! Vacation Bible
School with Colin on her hip.*

Laura with Colin at home, late October 2006

Laura with Colin and Cooper, just three weeks before she left this earth.

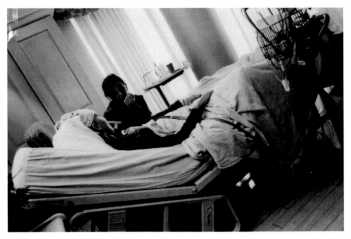

Laura and Vicki share a quiet moment at Menorah hospital

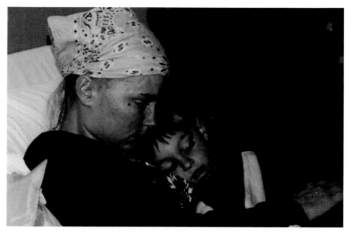

Laura with Cooper at Menorah hospital ... her final days.

Laura and her boys at the Broadmoor Hotel,
Colorado Springs, Colorado, October 2006

August 2005. Laura had experienced a grande mal sei-
zure on this day; came home, put on her "party" dress, and
attended a family wedding; Her strength, her perseverance,
and her faith are all showcased in this beautiful image.

Cooper and Colin, November 2007
Laura's greatest legacy, and the reason we remain
"prisoners of hope" *Zechariah 9:12 (NIV)*

listen|imagine|view|experience

AUDIO BOOK DOWNLOAD INCLUDED WITH THIS BOOK!

In your hands you hold a complete digital entertainment package. Besides purchasing the paper version of this book, this book includes a free download of the audio version of this book. Simply use the code listed below when visiting our website. Once downloaded to your computer, you can listen to the book through your computer's speakers, burn it to an audio CD or save the file to your portable music device (such as Apple's popular iPod) and listen on the go!

How to get your free audio book digital download:

1. Visit www.tatepublishing.com and click on the e|LIVE logo on the home page.
2. Enter the following coupon code:
   6007-9691-a9dc-f63e-4693-c848-6325-6d9d
3. Download the audio book from your e|LIVE digital locker and begin enjoying your new digital entertainment package today!